THE MORSEL OF THE STORY

Other Tasty Tidbits

by
The OBBC

Coatesville, Pennsylvania

THE MORSEL OF THE STORY
IS PUBLISHED BY THE OBBC
COATESVILLE, PA 19320

Copyright © 2013 by the OBBC

PRINTED IN THE UNITED STATES OF AMERICA

ALL RIGHTS RESERVED – No part of this book may be reproduced in any form without permission in writing from the publisher, except by a reviewer who wishes to quote brief passages in connection with a review.

Photography by Joyce Harpel

ISBN-10: 0615764673
ISBN-13: 978-0-615-76467-2

For Our Mothers

Our mothers gave us the wisdom to believe in ourselves.

They taught us that through love and kindness we would always succeed and that a sense of faith could pull us through the toughest of times.

We thank them for encouraging us to follow our hearts.

Millicent Regener Alexander

Alice Woodland Hill

Donna Hill McElwee

Elsie Mullen Mundy

Elsie Manetta Pilotti

MaggieLee Wilson Poole

Barbara Buckley Short

Lorraine Mott Stookey

Jennie Guiseppe Vietri

Acknowledgments

Bruce Mowday

Joyce Horn

Erik and Toni Campana

Corey Lee

Raymond and Lois Hinderling

OBBC Committee's Spouses and Family Members

Jen Osborn Redmile

David Grande

THE CHEFS

Laurie Cazille, President

Sue Young, Vice-President

Donna McElwee, Secretary

Cheryl Proudfoot, Treasurer

Gina Hove, Project Coordinator

Kelly Keyes

Cheryl Laurento

Euna Scott

Deb Patton

Table of Contents

Ingredients: A Look at What You Will Find in the Pages Within xi

Amuse Bouche: A Little Bite of Food to Amuse the Mouth
and Invigorate the Palate xv

The Morsel Of The Story 1

    Forbidden 3

    Forever Locked Away in Our Memories 13

    Unprotected 21

    Miracles Can Happen 29

    Faith + Trust = Confidence 35

    Lessons from History 43

    Unconditional Love 51

    Smitten 63

    Home Grown 75

    Not So Tasty 85

    A Picture is Worth a Thousand Words 93

    Imagine 101

    Self-Discovery 109

    Trapped 119

Piece de Resistance: The Best Part! 127

    Smarty Pants 129

    Pinkies Up, Please! 137

Leftovers 157

The OBBC Kitchen: Where to Find Our Recipes 164

Bon Appétit

INGREDIENTS

Ingredients is the inside look into the thinking of nine women who enjoy reading and eating their way through books. The purpose of **Ingredients** is to tell you about how the book is organized, give you some insight into the friendship and fun we have as a club, as well as what we discuss at our meetings.

The names of the different sections of this book represent a key element of our club; food. In addition to reading and discussing books, we also like to prepare meals for each other and never attend a meeting without introducing new recipes for club members to try. For this reason, you will find a word or phrase associated with food to describe the different sections and elements of the book. In turn, the ideas for the recipes for the meals were inspired by its theme or premise. (These recipes were either passed down from different family members or were unique creations made just to "try something new.") And the names of the recipes themselves are also all based upon characters and themes from these books.

Our book begins with **Amuse Bouche**, French for "mouth-amuser;" *a little bit* of food to amuse the mouth and invigorate the palate. An Amuse Bouche is usually served before the meal begins. In this section, you will meet The OBBC President who will tell you *a little bit* about our club, how we got started, and what this club has meant for all of its members.

The next section, entitled **The Morsel of the Story**, is an invitation to sit with The OBBC and to become part of a book club meeting. You will get a firsthand look at what we read, what we thought about the books we read, as well as other topics which became part of our discussions. You will also get to meet

THE MORSEL OF THE STORY

the members of the club. Each of the ladies has written an essay or two about how they may have been influenced by the reading of a particular book or how a certain passage reminded them of a special or personal memory. And, of course, you will get to see what we prepared, ate and drank at each of our meetings and how to prepare it yourself.

For each book we have read you will find 8 categories:

1. **Main Course:** The title and author of a book we read and discussed as a club.

2. **Food for Thought:** Thoughtful nourishment that we hope will spark interest in both reading the book and contemplating themes that go beyond its content.

3. **Culinary Critique:** Our club's synopsis and reflection of the book.

4. **Rating:** The clubs rating of each book on a scale of one to five spoons. The club rating is a calculation of the average submitted.

🥄🥄🥄🥄🥄 = **5** spoons: "I loved the book and I would read it again!"

🥄🥄🥄🥄 = **4** spoons: "I really liked this book and I would recommend it to others!"

🥄🥄🥄 = **3** spoons: "A good read!"

🥄🥄 = **2** spoons: "The book was O.K. Nothing special about it."

🥄 = **1** spoon: "I didn't like this book."

5. **<u>Seasoning</u>:** Other books, poems and/or personal stories related to the book we discussed.

6. **<u>Side Dish</u>:** A reflective essay written by one of the book club members.

7. **<u>a la Carte</u>:** A reference or major theme from a book which helped us to decide what recipes to prepare and serve at the book club meetings. Here you will find recipes for the beverages, meal starters, main courses and desserts which are great for book club meetings, special occasions and every day meals.

8. **<u>The Whine List</u>:** At each club meeting a new wine was tried. A comparison of wine to wit. The wine selected was intentionally paired with a quote or "whine" from one of the members during the club meeting. (Good thing someone was taking good minutes!)

The last section of the book describes two events which we organized after reading two wonderful books, one a classic and one a children's book. We call this section **Piece de Resistance**, the most important "dish." By sharing with you the recreation of these two favorites, you will understand our true love for reading. Re-writing the quote from Sir Francis Bacon...."Reading maketh a full (wo)man."

Lastly, you will find a section we call **Leftovers**. Leftovers consists of a collection of quotes taken from the minutes of our meetings which will have no particular meaning to you, the reader, but shows the lighter and zanier side of what went on during some of our meetings. (Yes, we do sometimes stray from the main topic.)

I am calling this meeting to order.

AMUSE BOUCHE

Welcome to our "novel" book club, The OBBC. We, as a book club, want to share with our readers how unique we really are. On the pages within, you are not only going to view some of the books from our reading list, but you are going to have the opportunity to meet each one of us in a special way, after which you will be invited to prepare and enjoy some of our own culinary creations.

The OBBC was created in 2009. Many of us were already meeting on a monthly basis to play cards until we decided to try something new. The craze for book clubs had come into vogue and we must admit we were hooked. The Oprah Winfrey Show opened a new door to reading which forced us to explore imaginative and sometimes provocative themes. She encouraged her audience to discover groundbreaking topics and encouraged us to look at books that we would not normally read. We learned that the only thing we had to lose was to stop turning the pages.

The OBBC, as a newly developed book club, embraced Oprah's challenge that "It's only when you make the process your goal that (a) big dream will follow." This inspired us with another idea to go beyond just reading. In 2010, we were determined to take what made us a special book club and become the ingredients that would create *"the perfect recipe"* and decided to write our own book.

We are a diverse group of women. Our ages range from thirty to eighty. What makes our book club so interesting is how differently we all think, feel and interpret books. We love to read and catch up on town events while enjoying each other's company. And, of course, we love to cook, bake and eat.

During the time we have been together as a club, we have opened our hearts to one another by sharing some of our deepest passions and fears, exposing our real selves. With each book we have read, we have grown even closer than we could have ever imagined. We have learned the true meaning of that old cliché, "you really can't judge a book by its cover."

In closing, I want to thank all members and non-members who made this dream of *The Morsel of the Story* a reality.

One more thing... We left out the secret ingredient; how we formed our name, The OBBC. We never disclose what the letters stand for and never tire of the imaginative ideas that friends and family come up with. If you have any suggestions, we would love to hear from you. You can send your thoughts to me, Laurie, at lcazille@live.com.

Laurie M. Cazille
Founder and President, The OBBC

The Morsel of The Story

FORBIDDEN

Main Course: *Twilight* by Stephanie Meyer

Food for Thought: What is eternity? How do you prepare for eternity?

Culinary Critique:

Prior to the reading of the *Twilight* saga, we all had the same idea about vampires; a living corpse who was eternally destined to prey ruthlessly upon others in order to survive. Whether we were into the modern day vampire introduced by the *True Blood* series by Charlaine Harris or the reminiscent creatures portrayed by acting legends such as Bela Legosi, we were in for something totally different. This story unfolds in Forks, Washington, where a coven of vampires known as the Cullen family resides. The *Twilight* series is the account of a cult of "vegetarian" vampires drinking only animal blood as opposed to human blood. They seek to live among their perceived victims and blend into the mainstream of activity of their community. The father of this extraordinary family is the well-respected local doctor who has five children who all attend the local high school.

But this is not merely a story about vampires and their life in a small town. There are a number of powerful themes found throughout the storyline: i.e. making life choices, temptation, immortality and love. Of these, we felt that the strongest theme was that of absolute love. In fact, we would not classify this book to be about vampires at all, but rather a love story. We were very easily swept away with the obsessive encounters and feelings of the hero and heroine. So much so, that we surprised each other by our interpretations of the meaning of love and its connection to our own personal lives. Disclosures of whom we were thinking as we read the romantic scenes made us all blush.

Edward and Bella came into each other's lives and experienced such an immediate emotional connection, they knew they could never be separated. Their intense passion and constant aching for one another became an overpowering force which outweighed all other values that had been established prior to their chance meeting.

Our favorite character was Edward. Even those of our group who were hoping for a more gothic and traditional portrayal of vampires were all enamored with Edward Cullen, who Bella described as "impossibly beautiful" and who we found to be an old world romantic.

After reading the 2,635 pages, (including *The Short Second Life of Bree Tanner*), most of us were left with but one question… when will the next installment be published?

The OBBC gives *Twilight* **4** spoons out of **5**.

Seasoning: Autumn Moon (Contributed by Sue Young)

From the moment of her discovery of Edward's true identity, Bella knows deep in her heart that at the tender age of seventeen, she has reached the Autumn of her human life. With only a few months before her prom, the event she hopes will usher in her immortal existence, she is ready to give up the beginning, the Spring, of what is to be her future as a mortal. Edward knows that if he goes along with her wishes to join him in a life of immortality, she will only have but a few short months to enjoy all that her human life has to offer.

Upon reading excerpts from a poem written by Sue's grandfather, John Regener, we could almost hear Edward's voice as he is torn between persuading Bella to change her mind or to take her to be his own.

Autumn Moon

You stand upon the hillside in the small hours of early morning
gazing in awe into the cloudless sky, the stars trying to outdo
the others in their small way in lovely splendor.

You stand spellbound and you cannot dictate to your conscience
but you know the surety that the hand that designed
this wonderful scene held a potential supremacy greater than mankind.

Autumn the defined meaning stands all out for decay,
the season of destruction, decline in the life of things we love.

Have we made each precious moment worthwhile?

Side Dish: Practical Principles by Gina Hove

One day while grocery shopping, I went down the book and magazine aisle in search of a new read. I started looking in the section of "bestsellers" and saw a book with a black cover on which were two hands that appeared to be holding out an apple to the perspective reader. The book was entitled Twilight *by Stephanie Meyer. I hadn't heard anything about this book, but the hands holding out the apple looked like a personal invitation to "take me." I purchased the book, satisfied that it was identified as a bestseller. After dinner that same evening, I opened to page one, and like many other fans of* Twilight*, was immediately hooked. As soon as I completed book one, it was off to the book store to purchase books two, three and four of the series.*

So what was it that attracted a 57-year old to be so intrigued and interested in a story intended for young teens? I believe that the answer to this question is simply that it **was** written for young teens. As a retired educator, having served 15 years in the classroom and 20 years as an administrator in the public school system, and presently working as an adjunct professor at a local university, my life has constantly been involved with young people. And the themes presented in Meyer's books address many of the issues with which my students, both then and now, struggle; developing a high level of ethics and good character.

An on-going theme that is found throughout the Twilight saga is how the characters deal with making choices. This story, even though filled with vampires, wolves, and special powers, focuses on the effects that decisions, whether long or short term, can have on one's life at the time of a decision, as well as on one's future. Meyer, in her books, as well as me in my classroom, strive to help students answer the question of how to make the right choice.

As was seen time after time throughout this saga, the characters don't always know if their choices are the right ones. Some are made by trial and error, and others are made by following one's heart. But in each situation, readers are presented with the process of making choices, all linked to that age old conflict of good vs. evil and in the end, making the right choice.

As we have all discovered, learning to make the right decisions sometimes takes practice. I am often asked by my graduate students to describe how they might help their own students make good decisions. Here is a simple plan which will work not only in the classroom but at home. On a page of notebook paper, ask your children to make four columns. In column one, have them list some of the toughest decisions they are presently facing. Then in column two, ask them to write why each decision is important to them. In column three, they should then write what they have done and are presently doing about each problem. Lastly, in column four, have them list new ways of dealing with these problems. This easy and straightforward process will not only help children "think before acting," but will open up a healthy and loving dialogue between teacher and student as well as parent and child.

Addressing and teaching ethical decision making should also be practiced in the classroom and needs to be emphasized in all schools and at all levels. I believe that teachers need to integrate into their daily lessons a set of standards that tells their students how they should conduct themselves. In addition to focusing on reading, writing, math, social studies and science, it is equally important for educators to emphasize standards of behavior that tell us how human beings ought to act in a variety of situations; as friends, family members and citizens. A person with strong ethical decision making skills will live a respectable and honorable life.

a la Carte:

Edward's "Red-Hot" Mushroom Turnovers:

When Edward is out to dinner with Bella, she orders mushroom ravioli. Sue took this idea and turned it into an appetizer. Instead of a pasta dish, she created a wonderful finger food; "red-hot" mushroom turnovers. (Sue thought Edward was gorgeous!)

EDWARD'S "RED-HOT" MUSHROOM TURNOVERS

8 oz. pkg. cream cheese – softened
1¼ cup plus 2 Tbs. flour
½ cup plus 3 Tbs. butter or margarine
½ lb. minced fresh mushrooms
1 small onion minced

¼ cup sour cream
1 tsp. salt
½ tsp. garlic powder
¼ tsp. thyme flakes
1 egg – beaten

In large bowl with mixer at high speed beat cream cheese, 1¼ cup flour and ½ cup butter or margarine until smooth. Shape into ball, wrap and refrigerate for 1 hour. In skillet over medium heat, heat 3 Tbs. of butter or margarine. Add mushrooms and onion and cook until tender. Stir in sour cream, salt, garlic powder, thyme and 2 Tbs. flour. Set aside. On floured surface, roll half of dough to ⅛ inch thick. Cut out circles with a 2¾ inch round cookie cutter. Preheat oven to 450 degrees. Spoon the filling onto one half of circle. Brush edges with the egg. Fold dough over filling. With fork, press edges and prick tops. Place on ungreased cookie sheet and brush remaining egg on the turnover. Follow the same directions for remaining dough. Bake for 12 to 14 minutes.

Pizza Dip Eclipse

Edward showed Bella that he could act like a mortal man by attempting to eat a slice of pizza. So ideas for pizza were incorporated into the meal for our club meeting. Getting an idea from a friend, Gina made a five cheese hot pizza dip and served it with crackers flavored with sea salt and olive oil. She added the word *Eclipse* to the name of the recipe as it was the title of the third book of the *Twilight Trilogy*.

PIZZA DIP ECLIPSE

- 8 oz. cream cheese
- ¼ cup parmesan cheese
- ½ cup cheddar cheese
- ¾ cup mozzarella cheese
- ½ cup Swiss cheese
- ½ cup provolone cheese
- green pepper, pepperoni, mushrooms, etc. (optional for toppings)
- 2 oz. DelGrosso New York style pizza sauce
- 2 oz. Scaramuzza's spaghetti sauce
- breadsticks or crackers

Mix cheeses together except mozzarella. Spread into a 9 inch pie plate. Mix pizza sauce and spaghetti sauce or use ½ cup of any desired pizza sauce. Pour over cheese mixture. Top with mozzarella cheese. If so desired, garnish with green pepper, pepperoni, mushrooms, etc. Bake at 350 degrees for 10-15 minutes. Serve with breadsticks or crackers.

Friday Night Special:

Bella's father's favorite meal was your classic "meat and potatoes." Laurie prepared for us the most unusual steak and potato dinner; she made steak and potato pizza. A recipe you just have to try! (Laurie confessed to us that she has become quite a connoisseur of pizza pie. It turns out that every Friday night, she "cleans out" the refrigerator of all of the leftovers from the week and creates a new pie. Now, that's creative cooking!)

FRIDAY NIGHT SPECIAL

approximately 3 russet potatoes
1 steak (fillet is a tender cut)
prepared pizza dough or box of pizza dough mix
A-1 steak sauce or one of your choosing
½ cup grated cheddar cheese

cornmeal – enough for rolling dough
salt and pepper to taste
1 Tbs. dried onion or 1 small onion - sliced
1 Tbs. garlic

Bake russet potatoes until done, usually 1 hour depending on size of potatoes. Set aside to cool before handling. Fry steak to blacken both sides to medium rare and cool. Use cornmeal for rolling out pizza dough and roll to a rectangular size to fit baking sheet or use a prepared pizza dough. Slice unpeeled potatoes into ½ inch pieces and place on top of dough. Slice steak in thin strips and add to top of potatoes. Add desired seasonings and steak sauce for moisture. Top with grated cheese. Bake at 350 degrees for 15-20 minutes until cheese is melted and crust is brown.

Forbidden Dessert:

On the front cover of the first installment of the *Twilight* series are two hands holding an apple. As you open the book, you are met with a quote from Genesis 2:17: "But of the tree of the knowledge of good and evil, thou shout not eat of it; for in the day that thou eatest thereof, thou shalt surely die."

Cheryl L. took the idea of this "forbidden" fruit and created an apple dessert which was sinfully delicious.

FORBIDDEN DESSERT

5 - 6 apples, peeled, cored and sliced
2 cups flour
1 cup sugar
1 Tbs. baking powder
2 eggs
¾ cup milk

1 stick of butter
2 tsp. cinnamon
½ tsp. nutmeg
1 small box of raisins
crushed walnuts

Preheat oven to 350 degrees. Melt butter and pour into 9 X 13 inch baking dish. Add apples and raisins and toss. Mix together ½ cup sugar, cinnamon and nutmeg. Pour over apples and stir. Mix flour and remaining ½ cup sugar with baking powder, eggs and milk. Top the apples with this mixture and sprinkle with crushed walnuts. Bake for 30 to 40 minutes or until brown on top.

From The Whine List:

After drinking a glass of *Verde Green Apple Sparkletini*, someone was heard to have said, "She's a two-timer."

FOREVER LOCKED IN OUR MEMORIES

Main Course: *Sarah's Key* by Tatiana de Rosnay

Food for Thought:

How could we have not known this?

Culinary Critique:

Prior to the reading of *Sarah's Key*, we were all familiar with the Holocaust and the Nazi's persecution and slaughter of the Jewish people. But we were all very surprised to read about France's role in World War II as it pertained to the Vel d'Hiv Roundup, the country's involvement in the deporting of thousands of Jews to Nazi death camps. Through the eyes of both an innocent child and a brave woman in search of truth, this novel brought to life the horrors and devastations of war in a way that we had never experienced.

Sarah's Key is composed of two interwoven story lines. One is of the viewpoint of Sarah, a young child and victim of the mass arrest of Jews in France in 1942. The other is of Julia Jarmond, an American journalist living in France, who in 2002 is asked to write an article about this "black day in France's past."

Julia is a writer for one of the local magazines and is given the assignment to report on the sixty-year old historical anniversary of the Vel d'Hiv Roundup. Not familiar with this particular piece of history, she launches an extensive investigation. What results is not a documentation of the events of a nation's past, but the story of a little girl named Sarah and her family, uncovering a secret which links this family to her own. And in Julia's persistence in following this story, we are able to retrace the footsteps of little Sarah, who is forced to live through what we have only read about, the killing of innocent people.

De Rosnay shares with her readers the brutality of Sarah's stay in an internment camp which proves to be unimportant when compared to the torment of this little girl's secret; a secret which can only be unlocked by the small metal key in her pocket. On July 16, 1942, in an attempt to save her younger brother from being arrested with the rest of her family, ten-year old Sarah locks him in their shared secret hiding place, giving him orders not to make a sound. After locking its entrance door and placing the key in her pocket, she promises to return in a few hours to let him out. But the hours turn into days.

The uniting force between Sarah and Julia is the bridging of the past with the present through the discovery of this secret place, a hidden cupboard. And the contents of this cupboard, so precious, come to symbolize the hearts and minds of a people unjustly persecuted; the harsh memory of a forgotten people.

Beyond the sad and haunting visions of the abuses endured by the French people, we could not help but focus our attention on the bravery and strength of the European Jewish population. We wondered if we, or our children, would be able to endure such a tragedy and asked ourselves, "Have we become desensitized by all of our privileges and freedoms?"

The reading of *Sarah's Key* was one way to keep the history of our world forever in our thoughts. It allowed us to do more than just add another book to our book club shelf. It gave us a distinct opportunity to experience the past, learn the truth and to remember those who suffered.

The OBBC gives *Sarah's Key* **5** spoons out of **5**.

Seasoning: In Her Words (Club Viewpoint)

More important than bringing history to life, historical fiction needs to begin a discussion of the key concepts of a particular era and its direct effect on altering the future. Of course, we do not suggest that this genre be used to substitute our history books, however, we believe that it can be a most significant resource in the discovery of the past. The overall content presented in *Sarah's Key* is indeed an important and powerful work of historical fiction. De Rosnay expertly weaves her story with the details from history which leaves you believing that every event of *Sarah's Key* could absolutely be true.

This story about the mass arrest of Jews in France sparked an interest in other works of literature related to this Nazi raid in Paris, carried out under the code name of Opération Vent Printanier or Operation Spring Breeze. Remembering our studies from high school, we went in search of a specific writing similar to that of *The Diary of Anne Frank*, the personal account of war seen through the eyes of a young thirteen year old girl. What we found was another such diary entitled *The Journal of Helene Berr*, a collection of the private thoughts and daily heartbreaking accounts of a young woman of 21 years. From her first day of having to wear the "yellow star" on her coat to her last entry, "Horror. Horror. Horror.," you will accompany her through her daily struggles and be amazed by her inner strength, and be introduced to a truly remarkable human being.

Our book club believes that this journal is a most significant resource in the discovery of the past and a true testimony to the human spirit.

Side Dish: I Will Never Forget by Euna Scott

The author of *Sarah's Key* states that this story is entirely fictional. However, the events that she described which occurred in Occupied France during the summer of 1942 are unfortunately true. By the reading of *Sarah's Key*, Euna, having lived during World War II, learned much more about the horrors which befell many innocent people. So many put to death with so very few who lived to tell their story.

What I remember most vividly about the 1940's and of World War II was the bombing of Pearl Harbor by the Japanese on December 7, 1941. My classmates and I were all called to our high school auditorium to listen to President Roosevelt announce on the radio that the United States was declaring war on Japan. I will never forget when in 1945 the United States dropped atomic bombs on Japan, resulting in its unconditional surrender.

When I think about the similarities and differences of all of the tragic events of the war, I can't help but think that the "roundup" of the Jewish families was the more agonizing. Indeed with the bombing of Pearl Harbor, Hiroshima and Nagasaki, many people died instantaneously. But in the Vel D'Hiv Roundup, the Jewish families were brutally treated day after day, all the while knowing they were eventually going to be put to death.

Like many other families of my neighborhood, during the forties, we didn't own a television. Some families did not even have a radio, nor did they have access to a newspaper on a regular basis. We all did our best to keep each other informed about the war. I remember one day skipping school and going with my friends to the cinema to see a movie. Not to a movie, really, but to see the newsreel. Back in the first half of the twentieth century, movies were all introduced by the playing of a newsreel, a short historical film reporting news and current affairs. On this particular day, I

Parkesburg Theater

watched a short film showing the shocking demise of children who died during the Holocaust. What will forever be engraved in my memory is the final scene in this documentary where Jewish children were lined up and shot. Everyone in the theater just sat there and sobbed. We were so overwhelmed and found it hard to believe this was really happening.

a la Carte:

"Locks" Cheesy Rounds:

The French are known for their breads and cheeses. Donna prepared crusts of bread covered with a blend of different cheeses and lox. (The word locks was added to the name of the recipe because of the word *key* in the title of the book.)

"LOCKS" CHEESY ROUNDS

2 cups sharp cheddar cheese
1 cup mozzarella cheese
½ cup butter
1 Tbs. fresh minced onions
1½ cup all purpose flour

½ tsp. salt
½ tsp. pepper
1 pkg. fresh lox (salmon) or tuna (optional)
sour cream (optional)

Using a mixer, beat together all the ingredients except salmon or tuna and sour cream until a dough ball forms. The dough will look shaggy. Chill dough for ½ hour in freezer. Roll out onto a clean, floured work surface and cut into rounds using a cookie cutter (about 1/8 inch thick). Arrange the cheese rounds on an ungreased baking sheet slightly apart. Bake at 400 degrees for 12-15 minutes until the rounds begin to brown on the edges. Allow them to cool slightly before serving. Optional – serve with sour cream and lox (salmon) or tuna.

Quiche La Clé:

As you might guess, a food mentioned in a story taking place in France would most likely be Quiche Lorraine. Cheryl P. baked this popular custard tart and named it La Clé, the French word for "The Key."

QUICHE LA CLÉ

1 9-inch unbaked pie crust
4 slices of bacon, fried and crumbled
4 eggs
1 cup half and half

¼ tsp. salt
⅛ tsp. black pepper
⅛ tsp. nutmeg
1 cup cheddar cheese

Sprinkle crumbled bacon in the bottom of the pie crust. Beat together eggs, half and half, salt, pepper and nutmeg. Pour the eggs over the bacon and sprinkle with cheese. Bake at 375 degrees for 45-50 minutes, until eggs are set in middle.

Tiramizoe:

Deb's recipe was named in honor of one of the character's (Zoe) first taste of Tiramisu.

TIRAMIZOE

1 cup coffee
1 Tbs. sugar
2 pkg. (3 oz.) ladyfingers, split and divided

2 pkg. (8 oz.) cream cheese, softened
½ cup sugar
2 cups thawed whipped topping
1 tsp. unsweetened cocoa powder

Combine coffee and 1 Tbs. sugar. Arrange 1 pkg. ladyfingers on bottom of 13 X 9 inch dish. Brush with ½ cup of coffee mixture. Beat cream cheese in large bowl with mixer until creamy. Add ½ cup sugar. Mix well. Whisk in whipped topping. Spread half the cream cheese mixture over the ladyfingers in dish. Top with remaining ladyfingers. Brush with remaining coffee mixture. Cover with remaining cream cheese mixture. Sprinkle with cocoa powder. Refrigerate 4 hours.

From The Whine List:

After drinking a glass of *Seven Deadly Sins Zins*, someone was heard to have said, "This is just one story. I wonder how many more are out there."

UNPROTECTED

Main Course: *The Blue Notebook* by James A. Levine

Food for Thought:

How safe is your neighborhood?

Culinary Critique:

When you first think about India, you may picture the beautiful Taj Mahal, one of the seven wonders of the world. Or perhaps, you would think about India's successful "Bollywood," the largest film industry in India, located in Mumbai. But through the eyes of 15 year-old Batuk, as seen in the writings she kept in a blue notebook, we see the horrifying existence of children who are forced to spend their young lives in the dark world of sexual slavery.

On assignment in India as part of his medical research, author James A. Levine, a doctor at the Mayo Clinic, interviewed some of the homeless children on the "Street of Cages" where child prostitutes work. It was during these interviews that he found a girl writing in a notebook. This gave him the motivation for his story; a story about a girl who records the thoughts and realities of her daily life on the Common Street of Mumbai, in a blue notebook. This note pad becomes her only escape from a life of prostitution, a life where she was forced to perform unspeakable acts in public where girls and boys, dressed as girls, are "trafficked."

During the few short years of her life, Batuk had hidden this diary in the mattress of her cage on the "Street of Cages" where she was boldly displayed by her "keeper." If not for this simple writing pad she would have nothing at all. From its first page to its last, she created a new and different world for herself.

The Blue Notebook gave us a raw and realistic glimpse of child prostitution. The intense details found within the pages of Batuk's notebook were so very lifelike that we not only struggled to read about her life, but also struggled to discuss it. Even though Levine's work is one of fiction, we were quite aware that this was a story of real life in Mumbai today, and an important story that needed to be told.

A strikingly sad story, *The Blue Notebook* was indeed the most emotional book any of us had ever read. And, the discussion that followed was equally emotional and expressive. Some found it too hard to accept the fact that a parent could sell their child into a life of exploitation; how a parent could be so shallow and materialistic. Others could accept the rationale of a family, so destitute, that they would have no other option than to sell one of their children in order to ensure the survival of the rest of the family.

The arguments presented through the discussion of this novel became so passionate and personal that members left the meeting feeling hurt, angry, and even outraged over viewpoints expressed. And it seemed that it was possible that the evening of June 20, 2011 could have been the end of our book club and worse, friendships among us.

Thankfully, we were able to refocus our attention on the fact that an important element of creating a successful book club was to allow all participants to share their opinions as well as to learn to appreciate all types of literature. We were reminded of our own by-laws which state that all members "have an opportunity to read book selections and express their thoughts and feelings through different perspectives... (and) there may be opposing points of view. Book discussions provide opportunities for participants to see the world through the eyes of the authors as well as other members of the group."

After days following the book club discussion and having time to think about Levine's purpose in sharing this story, we thank him for opening our minds to what can only be described as a courageous conversation on this issue.

The OBBC gives *The Blue Notebook* **3** spoons 🥄🥄🥄 out of **5**.

Seasoning: At Home or Abroad by Laurie Cazille

What could be more shocking than discovering that human trafficking happens not only across the globe but also in many of our small communities in the United States as well? The answer became Laurie's so-called "Ah-Ha" moment.

The images presented through The Blue Notebook were indescribably repelling, scenes that you might only see on the silver screen. They couldn't possibly be true. But knowing that what I was reading was based on fact left me feeling helpless. I was powerless to right what was wrong in another country so far away. So I directed my focus to our own homeland. I read a book entitled The Slave Next Door: Human Trafficking and Slavery in America Today *by Kevin Bales and Ron Soodalter, and what I found out came literally crashing down upon me.*

As the saying goes, "things happen for a reason." No sooner I began looking into this subject did a speaker come to my church for a special presentation on human trafficking in our country. "Impossible" was my only reaction as there is no longer slavery in America. But I learned that there are, in fact, slaves in America which can be bought for less than $100 and work as house, field or sex slaves with little to no pay and are beaten and shamed in unspeakable ways.

What I learned prompted me to sign a petition to support legislation for Bill 1310, The Trafficking Victims Protection Reauthorization Act. This will help to strengthen the laws to make Slave Owners accountable for their actions and get sent to prison. Although it sounds simple, I have learned it is not. To date, we have enabled this horrific crime by enforcing only mild penalties. Americans who are caught purchasing another human receive only a "slap on the back of the hand."

So I ask myself, now what. Finding what I can do to help remedy this problem in America has become for me a passion, my mission. But the idea of how to help the many victims is so overwhelming. I am involved at the local level and have become a volunteer with a local group to do whatever is needed to help victims.

As of August of 2012, I am pleased to report that our local law enforcement has been taking definitive action. Traffickers are being arrested in many local municipalities and in surrounding states. When I read about this in the newspaper I thought to myself that giving a little of one's extra time can speak volumes.

The subject of **Human Trafficking** *has made me become more aware of what is going on around me. I pay more attention to what I used to take for granted. And everything I learn on the way of completing my mission is also shared with members of our book club so that we can all make a small difference to end human trafficking in America and around the world.*

Here are two small but mighty ideas that our club tries to focus on daily. We are now informed consumers. We make an effort to find out where products come from and the conditions of those creating the products. And we keep our eyes and ears open. We look for evidence of possible human trafficking in the least likely of places. Below are three possible warning signs suggested by different anti-human trafficking organizations.

- *Evidence of physical restraint or assault, such as suspicious bruising.*

- *An overly controlling boss.*

- *A person who is always fearful and anxious.*

Following the reading of The Blue Notebook *and* The Slave Next Door, *we became more aware of an issue with which we could get involved and make a positive difference. To that end, we wanted to make you aware as well. Here is the National Trafficking Hotline: 1-888-373-7888.*

Side Dish: Imprisoned by Laurie Cazille

The Blue Notebook is a compelling story of a young girl's journey and her spirit of endurance. Knowing its content would be a "difficult read" for many of the club members, Laurie recommended this book to the club, not for shock value, but to increase our awareness of the "invisible" children of Mumbai, India. Here is her personal reflection.

I try to place myself in little Batuk's world and it is difficult. I try to relive one moment in the life of this nine-year-old girl. I go into my back yard and sit in my pet goat's pen, which is very small, trying to replicate in some way the daily life that has become the fate of this very young and beautiful child. I sit in the hay and straw. There is no visible opening except the gate. The smell of urine and feces linger in the heat of the day. I have made this goat pen, my "nest." My visitors are friendly and non-threatening.

I quickly realize that my attempt to duplicate Batuk's situation is inadequate. It is impossible to ever compare myself to the many children who have been sold like an animal; who have been forced to service the filth of humanity. I can't help but think of her fear and sense of abandonment having been sold by her father and never seeing her family again. I'm given to flashes of memory of a time when I was six-years old and while walking with my father, my hand slipped from his, and I was lost in the streets of Atlantic City. The sheer panic of not being able to find my dad is still vivid in my mind as if it happened yesterday.

In the telling of this story, Levine portrays Batuk as a very intelligent human being and I was intrigued with the analogies he used through this child to describe and endure her world. By the words and descriptions she used I was able to make a connection to her in the sense that she seemed to possess the core of who I am. Like Batuk, I have learned to grow into a person of strength and endurance with a thirst for knowledge.

I am a retired nurse and worked in a small county emergency department for over thirty years. Being a nurse had its rewards but it also had its difficulties. In the ER there were many times when I played an important part in saving someone's life and the feeling was amazing. Not so amazing, other times, my work required me to deal with children of abuse, neglect and rape, leaving me feeling so empty. I remember that the only way for me to cope with the horror and sadness was to work with law enforcement to help these cruelly mistreated children. Here in the United States there are laws to protect the innocent and consequences to be faced when an innocent child has been violated; not so in Mumbai.

This book touched me deeply and I was inspired by the courage of Dr. Levine to bring to his readers a world to where most members of our book club will never travel. It opened my eyes to important issues around the globe which need to be addressed. After I finished the book for the second time, I found a new perspective on my outlook on life. It opened my heart and made me thankful for the gift of my life chosen for me by God.

a la Carte:

Common Dahl Dip:

Dahl, a popular meal from India, was a new taste for all of us. After preparing dahl, Laurie combined it with sausage and served it with crusty French bread which made for an excellent appetizer. She named it after the street where the main character was held captive, Common Street.

COMMON DAHL DIP

4 cups vegetable broth
1½ cups yellow split peas
1 tsp. turmeric
¼ tsp. Cajun seasoning
½ tsp. salt
1 Tbs. butter
5 diced green onion

1½ tsp. cumin
pepper to taste
1½ tsp. ground cloves
½ lb. loose pork sausage
½ cup cheddar cheese
crackers or bread slices

Boil peas in vegetable broth. Add turmeric, Cajun seasoning, pepper and salt. Cook approximately 20 minutes. Fry green pepper and sausage in butter. Mix in cumin and cloves. Add to pea mixture and simmer for 4 - 6 minutes. Put in crock pot and warm. Serve in a bowl or dish. Top with cheddar cheese and serve with crackers or sliced crusty bread.

Tropical Cherry Sweet-Cakes:

There were many times in this book when sweet-cakes and pastries were part of the meals and so we chose to make this a major part of our get together to discuss the book. Cheryl L.'s sweet-cakes are combined with tropical flavors of coconut and pineapple soaked in coconut rum, topped with cherries and walnuts. The presentation of these cakes make for an elegant dessert.

TROPICAL CHERRY SWEET CAKES

1½ sticks of butter or margarine
1⅛ cup self-rising flour
3 eggs
3 Tbs. milk
¾ cup sugar
¾ tsp. baking powder
pinch of salt
½ cup chopped maraschino cherries

whole maraschino cherries for garnish
½ - ¾ cup coconut rum for soaking cherries
½ cup shredded coconut
½ cup crushed pineapple
½ cup chopped walnuts (optional)
½ cup confectioner sugar

Preheat oven to 375 degrees. Lightly grease muffin pan or use paper liners. Soak maraschino cherries in coconut rum. Reserve liquid for glaze. In a large bowl, combine eggs, sugar and margarine or butter. Beat together until smooth. In a medium bowl, mix together flour, baking powder, baking soda and salt. Blend into egg mixture. Stir in pineapple, cherries and coconut. Fill muffin cups. Bake for 20-25 minutes or until tops spring back when lightly touched. Mix confectioner sugar with the reserved coconut/cherry juice for glaze. When sweet cakes are cool, poke holes in top and spoon on glaze. Top with a cherry.

From The Whine List:

After drinking a glass of *Blue Point Old Howling Bastard*, someone was heard to have said, "That was the beginning of the nightmare."

MIRACLES CAN HAPPEN

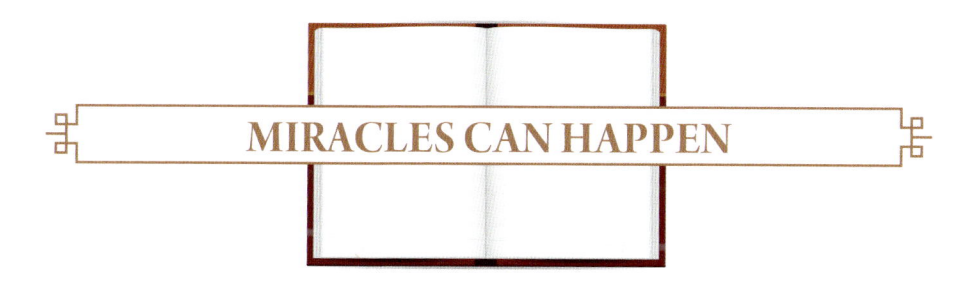

Main Course: *The Christmas Secret* by Donna VanLiere

Food for Thought:

Who's your jolly old elf?

Culinary Critique:

The Christmas Secret proved a perfect read during the winter holiday season as it allowed us to immerse ourselves in all the beautiful thoughts and feelings which surround us during times of tradition, and called to mind those deeply embedded beliefs of faith, hope and love. It was one of those stories which helped us to "recharge our batteries" by permitting us to put aside our worries and find joy in the most simple things in our lives. We learned from this short but touching novel, that the spirit of Christmas can sustain us through the most difficult of times.

Based upon what we garnered from reading *The Christmas Secret*, we offer our advice from a wise, old saying, "When you feel like giving up, remember why you held on for so long in the first place." ~ Unknown

The OBBC gives *The Christmas Secret* **4** spoons out of **5**.

The Morsel Of The Story

Seasoning: <u>Dear Santa</u> by Julia

Probably the best kept Christmas secret is the one we keep from our children, the one we wish we could keep forever; the reality of Santa Claus. In order to hold on to the magic of this "jolly old elf" for ourselves, we often keep our children's and grandchildren's letters written to Father Christmas. Here is a letter from one of "our" grandchildren:

> Dear Santa,
>
> How is the reindeer?
> My DaD said bi hum buge.
> By the way for christmas I wanta D.S.
> How are the prep and landing elfs?
>
> Your friend,
> Julia

Side Dish: The Doll in the Window by Cheryl Proudfoot

While reading *The Christmas Secret*, Cheryl was reminded of a special gift that she received one Christmas long ago.

This story reminded me of my own life as a child. My parents worked hard to keep a roof over my head and to provide for me. I grew up in a small steel town in the 1950's, during difficult times which were quite hard for everyone. However, I had wonderful parents and a wonderful childhood which I would not change for the world.

This story also reminded me of a special event that occurred on Christmas, a long time ago. My parents and my godmother took me on the train to Philadelphia to see all the holiday displays and decorations. While walking up and down the streets and gazing at all of the wonderful gifts in the store windows, a beautiful baby doll, dressed in elegant white lace caught my eye. I immediately fell in love with her. As you might guess, we left for home at the end of our trip without that doll as my father said we could not afford it. Not to worry, this was going to be an item that I would place on my Christmas list for Santa. But on Christmas morning, my doll was not under the tree. I couldn't help but wonder what I had done to make Santa think I was not a good girl. But later in the day I discovered that the reason Santa did not bring the doll was because he knew that someone else was going to bring her to me.

My godmother came to visit me on Christmas day and carried with her a lovely large package. And, in it was my doll, even more beautiful than when I saw her in the store window. My dear godmother had returned to the store to buy me that doll. I will treasure it always.

a la Carte:

Christmas Salsa:

In this tale of helping others at Christmas, packages were assembled with a variety of items, such as canned goods, to be shared with those in need. The mention of canned beans and corn led Laurie to prepare a bean and corn salsa to serve at our club meeting.

CHRISTMAS SALSA

3 scallions, chopped in small pieces
½ cup green pepper, chopped
½ cup corn
½ cup black beans

cherry tomatoes, desired amount
1 - 2 tsp. honey
2 Tbs. olive oil
1 Tbs. southwest seasoning

Chop scallions, green pepper and tomatoes (eliminate seeds). Add all ingredients. Refrigerate until ready to use. Serve with tortillas.

Holiday Chicken and Rice:

Each of us has a special meal we prepare during the holiday season. In this novel, the one mentioned is that of chicken and rice. Deb thought she would create this for the book club as a trial run to serve during the upcoming Christmas Season.

HOLIDAY CHICKEN AND RICE

1 can cream of chicken or cream of mushroom soup

1⅓ cups water

¾ cup uncooked regular long grain white rice

2 cups fresh or frozen vegetables

½ tsp. onion powder

4 skinless, boneless chicken breasts

½ cup shredded cheddar cheese

salt and pepper to taste

Stir the soup, water, rice, vegetables and onion powder in a 12 X 8 inch shallow baking dish. Top with chicken. Season chicken with salt and pepper as desired. Cover. Bake at 375 degrees for 45 minutes or until done. Top with cheese.

Santa's Jingles:

Is Santa real? The OBBC did not have to take sides with either of Christine's children, Zach or Gloria. We would simply have them set out a plate of Santa's Jingles and in the morning when they would see the empty plate they would know the reality of Mr. Claus.

SANTA'S JINGLES

¼ cup shortening
¼ cup butter
½ cup sugar
1 egg
1⅛ cups flour

¼ tsp. baking soda
½ tsp. salt
1 tsp. vanilla
red and green food coloring, colored sugar sprinkles, jimmies (optional)

Preheat oven to 350 degrees. Cream shortening, butter and sugar together. Add egg and vanilla. Stir in flour, soda and salt. Divide cookie dough in half – add red food coloring to one half and green to the other. Mix well. Drop by teaspoon full on to greased cookie sheet. Decorate with sugar sprinkles or jimmies and bake for 10 minutes or until done.

From The Whine List:

After drinking a glass of *Frog's Tooth Red Meritage,* someone was heard to have said, "I can whistle good without a tooth."

FAITH + TRUST = CONFIDENCE

Main Course: *Have a Little Faith* by Mitch Albom

Food for Thought:

Can another person be so connected to you that he or she could interpret your deepest thoughts and desires?

Culinary Critique:

People all over the globe are faced with a variety of trials and challenges. No matter their hardships and sufferings, they often are able to find an inner peace by turning to their faith. Whether one is deeply committed to a spiritual life or not, in times of trouble, it seems that by returning to one's core beliefs and rediscovering one's faith, solutions to life's trials can be found. The author of this tale helps us to discover that by trusting in something bigger than ourselves, we can come to a better understanding of our purpose here on earth. This story evidenced that no matter if one is Christian or Jew, our faith has a profound impact on our lives, each and every day.

Following the reading of *Have a Little Faith* we attempted to answer the question, *"What if our beliefs were not what divided us, but what pulled us together?"* We came to the conclusion that how we care for each other as human beings is more important than one's individual belief. Therefore, our only possible response was to become actively involved in reaching out to others.

Beginning with the next book club meeting, we began bringing food items, toiletries and cleaning supplies which would then be donated to a local food pantry and shelter in order to provide assistance to low income individuals and families. In between book club meetings we filled laundry baskets with household items that went to one of our local churches. We offered our spare change to fill baby bottles to give to that same church to help young unwed mothers. Last, but not least, we remembered that there were lots of other things to do…giving warm greetings to all we met, speaking kind words of encouragement to friends and family and visiting the sick.

The OBBC gives *Have A Little Faith* **3** spoons out of **5**.

Seasoning: Paula's Pocket by Gina Hove

Many of our first experiences with faith and trust occur when we are very young. Gina shared a story from her childhood which helped to shape her understanding of these two virtues.

My first understanding of the meaning of faith and trust came from an experience that goes back to when I was six years old. It was the fall of 1958 when during recess I saw another first grader, Paula, sitting on the school's steps crying. I left the game of "tag" that I was playing with my friends at the opposite end of the playground and went over to see what had caused her to be so sad. She told me that she had lost her pocket and was afraid to go home without it. My first reaction was to tell her how silly she was and say, "You can't lose a pocket; your uniform just doesn't have one!" But she was so upset and convinced she had it when she left for school, I offered to help her find it. (At that moment, I wondered who was sillier, Paula or me.)

To my surprise, her mood immediately changed. I was astonished by the amount of trust she had in my simple statement, "I'll help you find it." What I learned at that very instant was the power of kindness and its impact on trust and putting your faith in someone. I walked with her from one area of the play yard to the next, all the while saying to her, "Don't worry, we'll find it. If you lost it here in the playground, we'll find it!" and Paula followed me from corner to corner, with complete faith.

After about 15 minutes of unsuccessful searching, the bell rang and our recess ended. Our pocket quest had come quickly to a halt. Even though we never found Paula's pocket that day, she had stopped crying and was smiling; and so was I. What we did find was something more important that made a permanent impression on two first graders which would last for the rest of our lives.

Side Dish: Blessed by Donna McElwee

Have A Little Faith was a special read for Donna, especially because "Reb" reminded her so much of her late father whom she misses every day. Like Reb, he showed patience, wisdom, knowledge, respect, honor and faith in God. Donna tells her story...

After my mother passed away, my father had to take on all of the responsibilities of running the house. Now this was truly hard for a man who never cooked, cleaned, did laundry or any other everyday household job. Above all, his most important task was to continue to raise my wonderful sister, Geralyn, a child born with Down Syndrome. So, added to his new daily routine was seeing that she was kept mentally, physically and socially active on a daily basis. As difficult as this was, he excelled in every aspect of her care. But, over time, Geralyn became ill and my aging father could no longer meet the demands of caring for her. Sadly, she needed to be placed in a special facility and Daddy came to live with me and my husband.

Our new little family spent many happy hours watching television together, sharing stories and just enjoying each other's company. When I would knit, he would hold the yarn for me as I rolled it into a ball. It reminded him of my mother who used to crochet and I think it brought back some fond memories for him as he helped me.

Daddy was a great story teller. My family and I would sit and listen to him remembering his childhood, early adult years and his years in the military. Often, a neighbor would stop by just to hear a story or two. I regret that I never taped these stories because I would love to hear his voice again and revel in his storytelling. It would also be nice to pass his engaging tales along to the younger ones in the family who today only have a vague recollection of him.

My father fostered in me some of his wonderful traits as did Reb for Mitch. The one trait that had the most impact on me was faith in God. And, thanks to my Dad, my faith is strong. My father loved the Blessed Mother and went to St. Mary of the Assumption Catholic Church. (Until his dying day, he was devoted to her.) A few days before he died, he said, "You know, Donna, it won't be too long now." I responded, "I know, Daddy," but I knew in my heart that he would not be dying that day. The following day I received a call from the hospital telling me that he became unresponsive. I remember telling my sister that I believed he would not die until August 15, a few days away. When she asked me why, I reminded her that August 15 would be the Feast Day of the Assumption of the Blessed

Virgin Mary. Moving forward, we asked the hospital to call for a priest to administer the Sacrament of the Sick to my father. We did not request a specific priest, but to our surprise, the one who came, was from St. Mary's. Just as I had anticipated my dear father, Daddy, went home to God and his Mother Mary on August 15, The Feast of the Assumption.

Talk about a little faith....

a la Carte:

Oatmeal Dip and Honeydew Melon:

The description of Reb's clothes was quite unusual. So is the pairing of honeydew with oatmeal. Unusual, but delicious!

OATMEAL DIP AND HONEYDEW MELON

honeydew melon
1½ cups rolled oats
1 cup raisins
½ cup brown sugar

1½ cups milk
2 Tbs. honey
1 cup cold cereal of choice
sugar or artificial sweetener

Bring milk to a boil and add oatmeal. Add honey, brown sugar and raisins. Mix well and allow this to simmer for about 30 minutes. Stir occasionally. While oatmeal is cooking, slice honeydew melon in thin long slices eliminating the rind. Sprinkle melon with sugar or sweetener and refrigerate. Serve cold melon slices and room temperature oatmeal in a dipping bowl and top with cereal. (For best results, grind cereal into smaller pieces)

Reb's Seafood Pasta:

One of the themes we discussed after reading this book was how rituals and routines become important to connecting generations. We all agreed that one of most important of family routines occurs around the dinner table. Donna shared one of her customary meals, a seafood pasta with shrimp and tomatoes, that is good for keeping everyone at the dinner table for extended family time and long conversations.

REB'S SEAFOOD PASTA

1 lb. fettuccine noodles	dash of basil
1 bag frozen, cooked, deveined shrimp	dash of oregano
1 container cherry tomatoes	1 Tbs. parsley
1 bag spinach	parmesan cheese (optional)
2 cloves of garlic	extra virgin olive oil to coat shrimp

Cook fettuccine until al dente. Marinate shrimp in extra virgin olive oil and garlic. Steam shrimp. Combine all ingredients together. Add parmesan cheese (optional).

PB & G Bar Cookies:

Reb's culinary pleasures included graham crackers and peanut butter. Sue added graham crackers to one of her own cookie recipes and voila…

PB & G BAR COOKIES

1 cup flour
¼ cup crushed graham crackers
1 cup rolled oats
½ cup sugar
½ cup firmly packed brown sugar
½ tsp. baking soda

¼ tsp. salt
½ cup margarine or butter (softened)
½ cup peanut butter
½ tsp. vanilla
1 egg
1 cup chocolate morsels

Glaze -
  ⅓ cup powdered sugar
  3-5 tsp. milk
  2 Tbs. peanut butter

Mix all ingredients together except chocolate morsels and glaze ingredients. Press into a greased 9 X 13 inch pan. Bake at 350 degrees for 15-20 minutes. Sprinkle immediately with chocolate chips. Let stand for 5 minutes. Spread evenly. Mix powdered sugar, peanut butter and milk for the glaze. Drizzle or spread over chocolate frosting. Cut into squares.

From The Whine List: After drinking a glass of *Ghost Pines Merlot*, someone was heard to have said, "Your house smells like a funeral parlor."

LESSONS FROM HISTORY

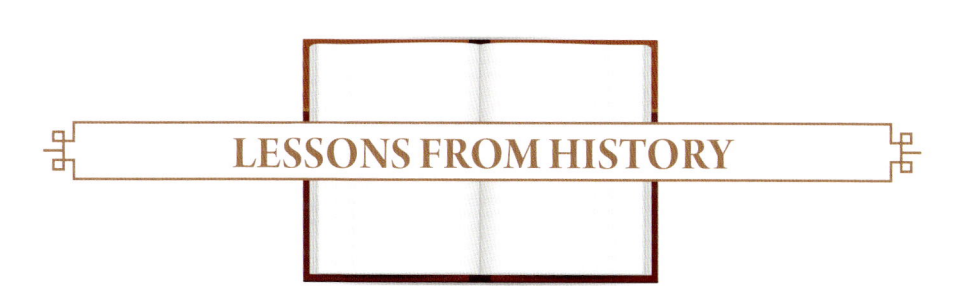

Main Course: *The Kitchen House* by Kathleen Grissom

Food for Thought:

Why do certain injustices continue throughout history?

Culinary Critique:

This story gave us a rich and authentic view of life and slavery on a tobacco plantation at the turn of the eighteenth century, as seen through the eyes of two main characters; seven-year-old Lavinia, orphaned while onboard a ship from Ireland, and her caretaker, Belle, the plantation master's illegitimate daughter. This profoundly touching story shows a young white skinned girl becoming genuinely bonded with her adopted black family.

Grissom's representations of the life of slaves added a deeper understanding to the history lessons we all remembered about the Colonial times and the inhumanity towards blacks, both adults and children. This story emphasized the reality that young black women were not and could not be protected as they were prohibited by law from defending themselves against abuse, sexual or otherwise, at the hands of white men.

Equally alarming was the realization that this culture of male domination was not reserved for black women alone. Lavinia, "the lady of the house," was given no more privilege than those given to the slaves.

This theme of injustice focused our attention on examining present times and we debated whether or not the hearts and minds of men had significantly changed since the eighteenth century. Without exception, we all believe that despite years of progress in the areas of acceptance and diversity, inequality still remains an issue in our country. In addition, fairness issues in the areas of gender, sex, mental and physical handicaps, race and ethnicity continue to be disputed on a daily basis.

After hours of dialogue, it is our consensus that if we, as Americans, want to take pride in our "melting pot" heritage, we must become a people of acceptance and truly live, love and celebrate our differences. As long as we see others through the eyes of prejudice, we will live in a society of fear, intolerance and injustice.

The OBBC gives *The Kitchen House* **6** spoons out of **5**.

Seasoning: Perspectives by Euna Scott and Kelly Keyes

As mentioned in the critique, the discussion following the reading of *The Kitchen House* was an personal exchange of ideas with many poignant comments made about the issues of integration then and now. Here are two annotations, one each from the eldest and youngest members of The OBBC, Euna and Kelly.

Euna: *When I was a young child I spent time with my grandparents on the eastern shores of Maryland. When I would walk on the sidewalk in our small town, a black person would have to get off and walk on the street. Also, many restaurants would not allow a "colored" person service and those that did would have restrooms designated "white" and "colored."*

Kelly: *We have come a long way since those days. Today we have a black president born to a white mother and a black father raised by a white grandmother. I am sure that it took both white and black votes to elect Barack Obama as President of these United States.*

Side Dish: The Christiana Riot Contributed by Euna Scott and Laurie Cazille

One of the members of the book club grew up near Christiana, Pennsylvania. She remembers that on one of the "back roads," in an Amish field, there was a blue marker. Every time she traveled this road she wondered about its significance until one day she decided to cross that field to investigate it. This marker spoke of *The Christiana Riot* which led her to explore its meaning and history.

On September 11, 1851, the first recorded open resistance to the 1850 Fugitive Slave Law occurred. A Maryland plantation owner, Edward Gorsuch, came to Christiana, Pennsylvania to retrieve four of his runaway slaves. (The 1850 federal Fugitive Slave Act gave rights to slave owners to retrieve their slaves and to have arrested those who protected them from recovery.) This is of particular interest to members of The OBBC as Christiana, located near the Lancaster-Chester County border in Pennsylvania, falls within a 25 mile radius from where we all live. This incident happened at the home of William Parker, an escaped slave. William Parker assisted runaway slaves to escape to Canada through the Underground Railroad.

Four men of the Quaker faith and 34 African American former slaves stood against the Maryland plantation owner and his son. In the end it was Gorsuch's own life that was lost. The events that followed this resistance divided the nation and less than ten years later the North and South were at war.

The marker is no longer standing, however the local historical society is going to replicate the Parker House as well as the marker in the town of Christiana.

*Members of the 3rd United States Colored Infantry Reenactors (l-r) –
Colored Sergeant Larry Harris, Private Antoine R. Watts and Private Joseph W. Becton*

a la Carte:

Plantation Cornbread and Cheese Casserole:

Like the people who lived on the southern plantation in *The Kitchen House,* Gina enjoys making and eating a variety of different versions of cornbread. Sometimes the bread is dry and crumbly and difficult to butter. But she discovered a recipe for making a cornbread casserole which bakes up moist and perfect every time. And one of the key ingredients is another one of her favorite foods, cheese!

PLANTATION CORNBREAD AND CHEESE CASSEROLE

---

4 oz. cream cheese, softened

¾ cup milk

3 eggs, beaten

1 can (15-½ oz.) whole kernel corn, drained

1 can (15 oz.) cream-style corn

1 pkg. (8-½ oz.) corn muffin mix

1 cup shredded cheddar cheese

2 oz. Velveeta cheese

2 oz. pepper jack cheese

Preheat oven to 350 degrees. Lightly grease a 9 x 13 inch baking dish. In a large bowl, whisk cream cheese and milk until smooth. Stir in remaining ingredients until well blended. Pour into baking dish. Bake 40 to 45 minutes or until golden brown.

Smokehouse Casserole:

Laurie was drawn by descriptions of black southern cuisine. She wanted to create a dish that was representative of those prepared during nineteenth century Virginia. One of the parts of the book which caught her attention was the long periods of time Papa and Ben spent in the smokehouse. This made her think of delicious smoked pork and ham. Laurie's smoked ham casserole recipe is perfect for hosting a group of "hungry readers."

SMOKEHOUSE CASSEROLE

1 – 2 lbs. smoked ham butt
1 small head of cabbage (shredded)
1 lb. small red bliss potatoes
½ lb. fresh green beans

bottle of Italian dressing
salt and pepper to taste
2 - 4 Tbs. butter

Bake ham for 3 hours in 200 degree oven. (wrap tightly in foil to represent a "fire spit"). Fry shredded cabbage in a skillet coated with butter. Season with dash of salt and pepper. Boil potatoes and green beans and add ½ cup of "ham flavoring" to the water. Cook until tender. Combine potatoes and green beans in casserole dish and sprinkle with ¼ bottle of Italian dressing. Slice ham and place on top of the casserole.

Millie's Molasses Cake:

The author shared with her readers the recipe for Molasses Cake. Sue shared with the book club her family's recipe handed down by her mother.

MILLIE'S MOLASSES CAKE

- ½ cup butter
- ⅓ cup packed brown sugar
- 1 large egg
- ½ cup milk
- ¾ cup molasses (mild flavor)
- 2 cups flour
- 1 tsp. baking soda
- 1 tsp. ground ginger
- 1 tsp. cinnamon
- 3 dashes ground cloves
- ¼ tsp. salt
- 1 Tbs. powdered sugar

Preheat oven to 350 degrees. Grease and flour an 8-inch square baking pan. In a large bowl, cream butter and sugar together. Beat in egg. In a separate bowl, mix milk and molasses. Combine flour, baking soda, salt and spices in an additional bowl. Mix in each of these mixtures to the butter mixture alternating, beating well each time. Spoon batter into the greased pan and bake for approximately 45 minutes or until a toothpick inserted comes out clean. When cool, sprinkle top with powdered sugar.

From The Whine List:

After drinking a glass of *Kitchen Sink White*, someone was heard to have said, "Next time bring the food that relates to the book." Then we heard, "What? We're not reading *The Help?*"

The Potluck Award

A potluck can be described in many ways. The definition by 16th century writer Thomas Nashe seemed to apply to our reaction to *The Kitchen House*. He used it to mean the "luck of the pot" or food provided for an "**unexpected** guest." No matter what book we read or discussed, an **unexpected** connection was made to what we garnered from Grissom's tale of loyalty, dependability and steadfastness. *The Kitchen House* was a powerful read and page turner from beginning to end. As a book club, not only did we give it our highest "spoon" rating but have designated for it a special award.

We give *The Kitchen House* our Potluck Award.

UNCONDITIONAL LOVE

Main Course: *Look Again* by Lisa Scottoline

Food for Thought:

What makes people turn and look the other way?

Culinary Critique:

We delighted in reading a book written by "a local girl." Making this book a special read was our familiarity with many of the names and places mentioned throughout the story, i.e. Narberth, West Chester, Valley Forge Park, etc.

Look Again is the story of a mother's love for her adopted son and her total commitment to his safety and welfare. When reporter Ellen Gleeson receives a "Have you seen this child?" flyer in the mail, she takes a quick glance at the photo and is about to throw it away. But she is strangely drawn to the image and looks at it again. The child in the photo bears a very strong resemblance to that of her adopted son, Will. All of her instincts as a journalist won't let her stop thinking about the photo and the possibility that her son may belong to someone else. She begins an extensive investigation which uncovers many secrets and heartaches, all the while unlocking the truth about her son.

Perhaps the most controversial aspect of our discussion was whether or not a single parent can effectively raise a child. Even though we all agreed that the best situation for children would be to have both a mother and father, we believe that there are sometimes circumstances that may not allow for this. If a single, loving individual can help to care for a needy and lonely child, the sacrifice of adopting a little boy or little girl is indeed one to be made.

The OBBC gives *Look Again* **3** spoons 🥄🥄🥄 out of **5**.

Seasoning: Short and Sweet

"It doesn't matter who you loved, or how you loved but that you have loved."
(Rod McKuen)

Side Dish: A Parent's Love by Kelly Keyes

"From the first page to the last page, I could not put this book down. I found myself staying awake until after midnight reading this book and then reaching for it first thing in the morning." - Kelly

I could not stop thinking what an unimaginable nightmare. I wondered what I would do. Would I take the easy way out and ignore the "have you seen this child" flyer, or would I want to learn the truth and investigate whether or not my adopted little son was that of a lost child whose parent was desperately trying to find him?

I was intrigued with the underlying topic, the question of parenthood and love. Does one need to be a child's biological parent to love that child? Where does the bond between a parent and child come from? This theme hit close to my heart. When I was two years old, my mother met the man who I call my Dad and always will. I have grown up loving and respecting my adopted father, and never once called him my step-dad. Based on the unconditional love that he has shown me all of my life, I believe that the bond between a parent and their adoptive child is as strong as the one between a biological parent and their child. In both cases, a bond is created that cannot be broken.

Unconditional Love

Daddy Jack married my mother when I was four and to this day I don't ever remember a time that I did not feel that I belonged to him. He provided for my mother and me a stable and secure environment. But most of all he has given me love and understanding. Growing up I could always count on him, whether it was dress shopping for the right outfit for my first dance or buying my first car. He was always ready and willing to lend an ear and shoulder as he counseled me on the best way to survive both high school and college.

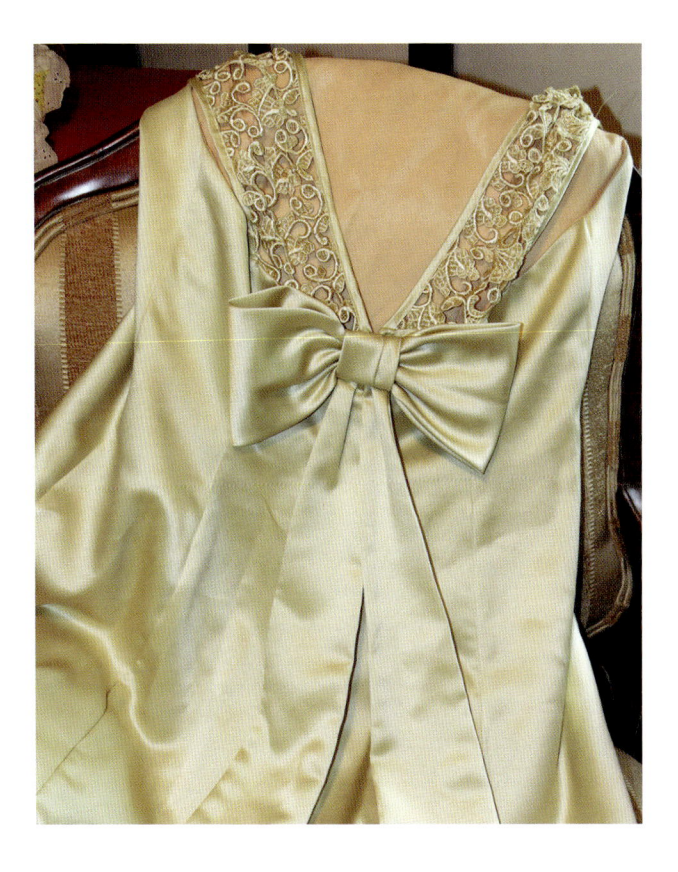

I could not have asked for a better father. I love him very much and I know he loves me. As I have become a mother myself, I find that the values he instilled in me are helping me become a good parent. How fortunate for my children that they have Poppy to be a part of their lives.

a la Carte:

Game Day Veggie Burgers:

Ellen and Will enjoyed playing games together. At break time vegetable burgers were the order of the day.

GAME DAY VEGGIE BURGERS

---

4 whole grain English muffins

8 Tbs. fresh salsa (Christmas Salsa found on page 32)

8 slices pepper-jack cheese

8 meatless burgers

brown mustard to taste

lettuce and tomato (optional)

Toast muffins, lightly butter. Fry burgers. Place burger on ½ of muffin. Top with cheese, salsa and mustard. Broil burgers to melt cheese.

Busy Day Chicken:

Kelly's idea for a main dish was inspired by Christine's very busy lifestyle. Having two active children herself, she understands the importance of making sure that no matter how busy a mom can be, preparing a hearty meal for her family must be fitted into her schedule. Kelly shared with us one of her fast and easy crock-pot meals.

BUSY DAY CHICKEN

olive oil

8 oz. boneless chicken thighs

½ bottle teriyaki sauce

¼ bottle of Asian ginger salad dressing

5 cloves minced garlic

1 white onion finely chopped

Set crock pot on low heat and coat bottom with olive oil. Place all ingredients in pot and cook for 5 to 6 hours stirring every half hour during the last 2 hours of cooking. Serve with rice.

Clued-In Jell-O Salad:

Green Jell-O is used as a possible clue to determine the identity of the missing child. Like most "kids" Will loved to eat this wiggly-colorful dessert. Sue prepared a green gelatin dessert that was cool, refreshing and delicious!

CLUED-IN JELL-O SALAD

3 oz. pkg. Jell-O gelatin lime or lemon
1½ cups boiling water
1 small can (8 ¾ oz. or smaller) crushed pineapple – not drained
1 cup shredded carrots

2 oz. softened cream cheese
1 cup Cool Whip
3 Tbs. sugar
½ cup crushed walnuts or pecans (optional)

Dissolve Jell-O gelatin in boiling water. Add pineapple – not drained. Chill until thick. Fold in carrots and pour into a 9 X 9 pan or glass casserole dish. Chill until firm. Mix cream cheese, cool whip and sugar together and spread on top of gelatin mixture. Sprinkle with nuts.

Snicker Brownies:

At dinner one evening at the end of the story, Ellen's fiancé equated Snicker bars to romance. (Like the old adage says, "the way to a man's heart is through his stomach.") There are many recipes today that use candy bars for ingredients. Donna added Snickers to her favorite recipe for brownies.

SNICKER BROWNIES

prepared brownie mix – cooled
Hershey's chocolate frosting
1 stick of butter or margarine
⅔ cup Hershey's cocoa powder

3 cups powdered sugar
⅓ cup milk
1 tsp. vanilla extract
Snickers candy

Melt butter or margarine in saucepan. Stir in cocoa powder. Add sugar and milk alternating a little at a time. Beat the mixture to a spreading consistency adding a small amount of milk if necessary. Stir in vanilla extract. Spread frosting on top of brownies and add crushed or chopped Snickers candy.

From The Whine List:

After drinking a glass of *Dialed In Red*, someone was heard to have said, "Didn't they check for DNA?"

Bon Appétit

Bon Appétit

— STARTERS —

Christmas Salsa.. 32

Common Dahl Dip.. 27

Cornfield Chowder.. 79

Edward's "Red-Hot" Mushroom Turnovers................................... 8

Insane Artichoke Dip.. 124

"Locks" Cheesy Rounds 17

Oatmeal Dip and Honeydew Melon... 39

Pizza Dip Eclipse... 9

R & C Seafood Chowder.. 106

Shore Crab Dip.. 69

— BEVERAGES —

First Date... 70

Six Pack Punch.. 80

Tatted-Up Coffee... 97

— SIDES —

Collector's Baked Beans... 71

James' Special Slaw.. 114

Pepperoni Potato Casserole... 89

Plantation Cornbread and Cheese Casserole................................ 47

Bon Appétit

— ENTREES —

Austen-Tatious Oysters 144

Busy Day Chicken 55

Carrot Raisin Tea Sandwiches 142

Cucumber Sandwiches with Mint Butter 140

Dale's Breakfast Delight 81

Elsie's Luncheonette 98

English Toast Casserole 115

Friday Night Special 10

Game Day Veggie Burgers 54

Hero Bacon Quiche 72

Holiday Chicken and Rice 33

King's Roast on Toast 82

Mellow Yellow Chicken & Squash 125

Petticoat Chicken Cups 143

Postman's Pasta Bake 73

Quiche La Cle' 18

Reb's Seafood Pasta 40

Smokehouse Casserole 48

Tumbon 90

Walnut Tea Sandwiches 141

Bon Appétit

— DESSERTS —

Backup Apple Crisp 117

Chair Man's Lemon Trifle 91

Clued-In Jell-O Salad 56

Drive Thru Lemon Sponge Pie 116

Forbidden Dessert 11

Keepsake Apple Dip 146

Melt in Your Mouth Scones 108

Millie's Molasses Cake 49

PB & G Bar Cookies 41

Sacred Triple Chocolate Brownies 107

Santa's Jingles 34

Snicker Brownies 57

Stottsville Graveyard Pudding 83

Strawberries and Balsamic Vinegar 145

Tiramizoe 19

Tropical Cherry Sweet Cakes 28

Twisted Pretzel Pineapple Salad 126

SMITTEN

Main Course: *Dear John* by Nicholas Sparks

Food for Thought:

What if the feeling of "love at first sight" could last forever?

Culinary Critique:

Before beginning to read this novel, we all assumed that it would be your "run of the mill" romance story. Special Forces Army Sergeant John Tyree, home on leave from his most recent military assignment, meets Savannah Curtis, a college student at the University of North Carolina, and is smitten. As is expected, both fall in love at first sight. But to everyone's surprise, the main ingredient for a typical love story is missing. There is no "and they lived happily ever after." Even though the love between Savannah and John at first appears to be permanent and deep, a conflict develops which is never resolved. John's commitment to country first is chosen over his love for Savannah.

Dear John is not your classic "boy meets girl" love story, but a tale about responsibility and courage. Sparks leads the reader through a development of a young man's character that grows from someone who is indifferent and apathetic to life, to someone who willingly sells his only fortune to save the life of another.

As the story unfolds, you will see a transformation occur in both of the two main characters as their relationship grows. John's temperament and attitudes about life change from pessimism to optimism. Savannah, who in the beginning of the story works to inspire John with her free spirit and passion, grows passive and indifferent.

In the end, John and Savannah do not live happily ever after, for they both abandon love… not what we expected.

The OBBC gives *Dear John* **3** spoons out of **5**.

Seasoning: To Mom (Contributed by Cheryl Laurento)

During our discussion of *Dear John* we talked about the many stories, books and movies of lovers corresponding by mail during times of war. Like the title suggested, we focused on the conventional "Dear John" letters, those letters resulting in many broken hearts. But what about the letters sent in hopes of deepening relationships? What about all of the beautifully penned love poems? What about the ones we ourselves had written and received? Cheryl L. shared a love poem that was written by her grandfather, George Stookey, to his wife, Ida, during his retirement years. It is entitled, "To Mom."

To Mom

Oh I had loved a dozen girls
And all of them were fine
But never did quite get the urge
To make one of them mine.

But the first time I met MOM
I fell in love with her
And got those blithesome dizzy spells
That kept me in a whir.

And every day and hour dragged
in never ending train
Delaying endlessly the time
When I'd see her again.

And finally there came the day
At long distressing last
When she loved me too and answered yes
And we married good and fast.

And so it's been through many years
Through fortune good and bad
I've stood by her and she by me
And a happy life we've had.

And I've loved her and she's loved me
And our children all love us
Grandchildren too -- a multitude
Over us make a fuss.

Just why it's so I cannot say
And I feel that I'm life's debtor
For every day I'm with her now
I love her more and better.

The Morsel Of The Story

Side Dish: <u>Postmarked</u> by Sue Young

Sue identified many connections with John Tyree, and wanted to personally share some of them with him....so she wrote him a letter.

Dear John,

I just finished reading the book written about you and your life by author Nicholas Sparks. I enjoyed it very much and I found that a lot in the book is similar to my life. As a child, I can remember sitting with my father looking through coins that he would bring home every day. He scanned each coin looking for the date and mint mark and placed it in a specific coin collector's book. He had a wonderful collection. My favorite were the Buffalo Nickels and the Indian Head Pennies. As the years went on, my father presented my sister and me with completed coin books and later gave some to his grandchildren. My son, Dan, is an avid coin collector today. I know my father and Dan would have loved to have spent time looking through and discussing coins with your father. And coincidently, my son is also a mail carrier. Maybe there would have been a few postal stories shared between your father and him.

When you met Savannah, it reminded me of when I met my husband, Bruce. We lived in the same area growing up, but our paths never crossed. We met on the beach in Ocean City, NJ. He spotted my beach towel which had our high school's mascot printed on it. Bruce & his friend asked if I was from Coatesville. I answered yes, we exchanged some small talk, and I never saw Bruce again until months later. Funny how some people meet the ones who they will spend the rest of their lives with!!!

I find it hard to believe that no one who was with Savannah the day you met her didn't even try to retrieve her bag that had fallen into the ocean. I know how upset she must have been. Her purse, her pictures, money, keys... all possibly gone until you dove in to find the bag. I can appreciate how she felt from an experience of my own. A few years ago, my purse didn't fall in the ocean or lake but it plunged into a toilet in a local bowling center...by accident. (You probably didn't need or care to hear about that funny episode, but Savannah's bag falling into the water reminded me of my funny but sad dilemma.) I retrieved my possessions to find that everything was o.k., all but the purse that later went into the trash can...on purpose.

Growing up for you must have been a huge challenge. Your parents separating and having a father with Asperger's Syndrome had to be tough. Of course, you didn't know in your early years what your dad was living through. And he did all he could do for you while holding down a great job. In our family, we have become more aware of Asperger's. There are mild to severe symptoms that a person can show. We learned that love and patience go hand and hand.

John, it is obvious to me that the love for your country played a major part in your life. Choosing between serving more time in the army during our country's greatest time of need or coming home to stay with Savannah... how does one make this tough decision? My father, James W. Alexander, served in the United States Army Fifth Air Force during World War II from 1941 through 1945. He was a technical sergeant on a B-24 bomber, The Yankee Doodle Dandy of the Jolly Roger's 90th Bombardment Group. He also loved serving his country as you did. During his training, there was an accident in Salina, Kansas. The bomber plane was forced to make a crash landing and my father along with another crew member bailed out and parachuted to safety. Two others were not so fortunate. One lost his life and the other was critically injured. My dad entered a hospital for a short stay then was released to join a new crew and return to his service. He witnessed just in his training what most of us will never have to see or endure in our lifetime. He later went on to serve in the war in the South Pacific Theater taking part in more than two hundred hours of bombing missions. His courage, faithfulness and devotion to The United Stated of America's Armed Forces was so strong.

Thank you Dad, John and all who have served and are currently serving in our armed forces. You are our heroes and we salute you!

Dear John, I hope this letter finds you well, that you are leading a happy, prosperous life and have found another one to love. God Bless!

Take care,
Susan Young

a la Carte:

Shore Crab Dip:

Sue's idea for this recipe was based on the reference made to the beach found in Chapters 2 and 3. Here in Pennsylvania, we refer going to the "beach" as going to the "shore."

SHORE CRAB DIP

3 Tbs. margarine or butter
2 Tbs. finely chopped onion
2 Tbs. flour
¾ cup shredded Monterey jack cheese
¾ cup shredded sharp cheddar cheese
8 oz. can lump crab meat

1 (13 oz.) can evaporated milk
2 drops of Tabasco sauce
salt and pepper to taste
loaf of pumpernickel bread (optional)
crackers of choice (optional)

Sauté onion in margarine or butter in a 1½ or 2 qt. saucepan. Add flour. Remove from heat and stir in evaporated milk. Heat slowly to slightly thicken. Add cheeses and crab. Stir enough to thoroughly mix and melt cheeses. Season with Tabasco sauce, salt and pepper to taste. Serve crab dip in a bowl with crackers or pumpernickel bread, hollowed out, using reserved bread pieces for dipping. Dip can be reheated in microwave.

First Date:

When Savannah and John go out on their first dinner date together, they both order iced tea, as Savannah states that she doesn't drink alcohol. Since this date took place in the summer, Gina mixed a non-alcoholic cooler to commemorate the couples' first date.

FIRST DATE

maraschino cherries
crushed ice

white cranberry/peach juice
orange juice

Drop a cherry in a wine flute. Fill glass with ice. Fill half the glass with white cranberry/peach juice. Fill the remainder of the glass with orange juice. Avoid stirring the drink. Let the cranberry juice slowly mix with the orange juice.

Collectors Baked Beans:

We learned that a frequent meal of John and his father was that of hot dogs and baked beans, so Sue prepared a baked bean recipe enjoyed by her family. Since an important connection between John and his father was a coin collection, she named it Collector's Baked Beans.

COLLECTOR'S BAKED BEANS

- 7 slices of bacon
- ½ lb. ground beef
- ¼ cup finely chopped onion
- ½ cup catsup
- 1 tsp. salt
- ½ cup firmly packed brown sugar

- 1 tsp. dry mustard
- 1 tsp. vinegar
- 1 can kidney beans
- 1 can pork and beans
- 1 can northern beans
- 1 can butter beans

Cook bacon in large skillet until crisp. Drain bacon on a paper towel. Crumble when cool. Cook beef in fat remaining in skillet. Add onion and sauté until tender. Combine the beef and onion with catsup, salt, vinegar, brown sugar and mustard in a 3 quart baking dish. Partially drain all beans and add to baking dish. Stir gently to mix. Bake at 350 degrees for 40 minutes. Sprinkle with bacon and enjoy!

Hero Bacon Quiche:

The morning after they met, John made a simple bacon and egg breakfast for Savannah. Donna baked for us a bacon quiche and named it in honor of John, a real hero.

HERO BACON QUICHE

6 large eggs
1½ cups heavy cream
salt and pepper to taste
2 cups chopped fresh baby spinach

1 lb. bacon
1½ cups shredded Swiss cheese
1 (9-inch) refrigerated pie crust

Preheat oven to 375 degrees. Combine eggs, cream, salt and pepper in a food processor or blender. In the bottom of a 9-inch pie plate, fit the crust to the plate and layer spinach, bacon and cheese. Pour egg mixture on top. Bake for 35-40 minutes until egg mixture is set. Cut into 8 wedges.

Postman's Pasta Bake:

John's father's idea for spaghetti sounded like a good one for a book club meeting. Baked pasta was just what we needed to keep the conversation moving as we discussed this month's pick.

POSTMAN'S PASTA BAKE

- 1 lb. linguini
- 1 (16 oz.) jar Prego three cheese spaghetti sauce
- 1 lb. mushrooms, sliced
- 16 oz. ricotta cheese
- 1 pkg. shredded mozzarella cheese
- 5 oz. grated parmesan

- 1 lb. loose Italian sausage
- ½ tsp. basil
- ½ tsp. oregano
- olive oil to coat pan
- salt and pepper to taste
- 2 Tbs. red wine
- 2 Tbs. butter

Boil noodles according to instructions on label and set aside in large bowl. Drizzle with olive oil to prevent sticking. Add parmesan cheese. Sauté mushrooms in butter and red wine until done. Fry loose sausage in olive oil and add to spaghetti sauce. Add basil, oregano, salt and pepper to taste. In 13 X 9 inch or larger casserole dish, cover bottom with ½ of the sauce. Layer linguini, cooked mushrooms, ricotta cheese and ⅓ of the mozzarella cheese. Repeat layering and top with remaining sauce, sausage and mozzarella cheese. Bake at 350 degrees for approximately 30 minutes or until bubbly. Slice in squares and serve.

From The Whine List:

After drinking a glass of *Barefoot Cellars Riesling,* someone was heard to have said, "Salvia!? What!? You can buy it on the boardwalk?"

HOME GROWN

Main Course: *Jailing The Johnston Gang* by Bruce Mowday

Food for Thought:

Does the punishment always fit the crime?

Culinary Critique:

The local landmarks and hometown "celebrities" found in *Jailing The Johnston Gang* were the drawing cards for most of us to keep the pages turning on this popular work of nonfiction. The saga of the Johnston Gang became well known even via the silver screen. Even though much of the "neighborhood" as we remember has vanished, the telling of a true story circa 1960 and 1970 brought back many memories of Coatesville and its surrounding areas.

Pennsylvania's Johnston Gang was led by Bruce Johnston Sr. and his brothers, Norman and David. They formed the nucleus of a burglary ring and made millions of dollars. They eventually added murder to their crimes with the killing of two police officers in 1972 and four of the youngest members of the gang who they feared were going to "rat them out" in 1977 and 1978. These crimes also included the attempted murder of Bruce Sr.'s own son.

We all expressed our admiration for the dedication of the law enforcement who often times were not paid for going above and beyond the call of duty in order to crack this ring of thieves and murderers. Their passion to stick with this case no matter what the stumbling blocks, demonstrated their strong sense of doing the right thing for the communities they represented.

After meeting the author, Bruce Mowday, we were impressed with his dedication as well. We didn't realize the tremendous amount of detailing that went beyond what was written in the newspapers. Mr. Mowday fulfilled our reading expectations as this moment in history was keenly documented and presented. His attention to detail brought us more than just the facts of the case, but gave us an insight into the families, friends and victims whose lives were forever changed by the events surrounding this crime spree.

The OBBC gives *Jailing the Johnston Gang* **4** spoons 🥄🥄🥄🥄 out of **5**.

Seasoning: Our Inspiration (Club Viewpoint)

As mentioned above, we were very honored to have the author of *Jailing The Johnston Gang*, Bruce Mowday, come to one of our book club meetings. His captivating "behind the scenes" details were told with skill and precision, leaving us with images of this unforgettable story.

He is both a very knowledgeable person and accomplished author and we have put other books from his collection on our "must read" list. Next up, *Richie Ashburn ... Why The Hall Not: The Amazing Journey to Cooperstown* and *Life With Flavor: A Personal History Of Herr's*.

Chester County Detective Anthony Massarotti, Sue Young and Bruce Mowday

Side Dish: I Wonder by Deb Patton

Bruce, David and Norman Johnston helped themselves to anything that wasn't nailed down. From the mid-1960's through the next decade, it was common knowledge that they stole antiques, diamonds, gold, silver, tires, farm equipment and lawn tractors. They hijacked trucks filled with groceries, cigarettes and pantyhose. They even robbed Dutch Wonderland Amusement Park and Longwood Gardens, popular local attractions which I often visited.

I can only imagine that without my knowing it, I was part of their setting as I also frequented many of their favorite "watering holes" and "hangouts." I never realized until after I read Jailing The Johnston Gang *that I could have bumped into them on any given day... or night.*

Fast cars and new freedoms are both part of my memories of the late 1960's. I had a '68 Camaro and spent every cent of my paycheck at Sielski's Speed Shop in Thorndale. Could I have been standing in the speed shop when the Johnstons were there? I wonder.

The Morsel Of The Story

I enjoyed going to the Anvil Inn in Kennett Square to meet up with friends and party. Could I have been standing with one of the Johnston Gang there? I wonder.

This was all a possibility as even some of my friends had direct encounters with some of their capers. For example, in 1972, my friend, Laurie, was working in the emergency room of Chester County Hospital when two Kennett Square officers were brought in. As was described in Mowday's account of this band of thieves turned murderers, both officers were shot in the back by members of this homegrown notorious gang. For me, it was almost unbelievable to think that a close friend had to deal with the aftermath of the unspeakable crimes of men whose names were synonymous with the Coatesville area.

A favorite place for the Johnston Gang to meet was the Stottsville Inn. I worked there for a number of years. I often wonder if I ever served one of the Johnston Gang. I wonder if while traveling to and from work I passed them on one of those back roads as they were trying to dispose of any of their victims.

It seems like only yesterday that the Johnstons and their accomplices were tried and jailed and I continue to this day to follow the stories of their escapes and appeals. Recently, I attended Bruce Mowday's book review held at the Stottsville Inn. Several of the victim's family members as well as relatives of the Johnston's family attended. It was a very somber and sobering event. Meeting these people and listening to their stories had a tremendous impact on me. It was more powerful than any movie or book ...it was REAL LIFE!

My fascination with a "real" crime that was ever so close to me continues to this day. Jailing The Johnston Gang sits on a shelf in my room along with the over glorified movie on the same subject, "At Close Range." (My favorite actor is Christopher Walken, who in the movie did a wonderful job of making an evil man look good.)

a la Carte:

Cornfield Chowder:

"Mitchell led Cloud and county detective Larry Dampman down a tractor path and through several cornfields to the grave site."

Cheryl P. took this line from the story to make us corn chowder. This is a great crock-pot recipe which can be easily prepared!

CORNFIELD CHOWDER

¾ cup chopped onion
3 Tbs. butter or margarine
2½ cups frozen southern style hash browns
1 cup diced cooked ham
1 - 16 oz. pkg. frozen corn

3 cans of creamed corn
1 can cream of mushroom soup
1 can cream of celery soup
5 cups milk
salt and pepper to taste
pinch of parsley

Combine all ingredients in crock pot. Cook on high for 4 - 5 hours. (This recipe prepares for a large group. For smaller amount, cut the recipe in half.)

Six Pack Punch:

With quite a few references to bars and taverns, Kelly decided to make a beer punch. Preferring wine to beer, the group was a bit skeptical at first but found it to be wonderful and refreshing.

SIX PACK PUNCH

2 liters prepared lemonade
½ gallon rainbow sherbet
3 (16 oz.) cans of beer (your choice)

Combine lemonade and beer into a punch bowl or large pitcher. Scoop the sherbet into bowl/pitcher to float on top. Allow it to melt into the liquid.

Dale's Breakfast Delight:

"Richter also told a story about Dale (one of the main characters in this story of theft and murder) ordering breakfast. 'One day Leslie wanted to order breakfast and we said he could. So he called 7:00 or 8:00 A. M. and asked for room service. He said he wanted two eggs, the white part really burnt and the yolk real runny, and the toast black and the bacon done so when you touch it, it breaks up. The waitress said she wasn't sure if we could prepare the order as Dale ordered. Leslie said, Why not? You did it yesterday.'"

At the night of our book club meeting, Sue prepared for us her rendition of Dale's breakfast.

DALE'S BREAKFAST DELIGHT

6 eggs, beaten

5 strips bacon, fried crisp

3 slices cheddar or American cheese

4 very thin slices of well done toast

¼ cup milk

1 tsp. butter or cooking spray

Fry bacon until crisp. Cut up into 2 inch pieces. In a large frying pan, melt butter or coat with cooking spray. Pour eggs, milk and cooked bacon in pan to scramble. Place in a 9 X 9 casserole dish. Put cheese on top and melt in oven or microwave for a few minutes. Cut toast into 4 pieces and place in sides of casserole dish.

Kings Roast on Toast:

"One night Dampman investigated what seemed to be a run-of-the-mill argument among some patrons at a Downingtown diner. Dampman charged three of the men with disorderly conduct and they were released. Within days of the charges, August 18, 1970, one of the men, John William "Jackie" Baen of Coatesville, was found dead, floating in the west branch of the Brandywine River at McCorkles' Rock near the King Ranch. At the time the famous King Ranch of Texas was affiliated with a cattle operation in Chester County."

Texas is indeed noted for their wide variety of beef dishes. Here in the east, we are proud of our hot roast beef sandwiches; easy to serve up for any occasion.

KING'S ROAST ON TOAST

3 to 4 lb. eye roast
salt and pepper rub
toasted Kaiser rolls

horseradish
American cheese or cheese of choice

Bake eye roast, seasoned with a salt and pepper rub, uncovered for approximately 1-2 hours. Cook until it is crusty brown on the outside. Let the meat cool before slicing. Add water to the meat drippings in a saucepan and bring to a boil. Set aside. Slice roast beef into thin pieces and place in a crock pot with the beef juice. Simmer for 1 hour. Serve on Kaiser rolls with a slice of cheese and horseradish to taste.

Stottsville Graveyard Pudding:

Cheryl L.'s inspiration for this dessert came from the sections in the book where graves were found. "At 8:10 P.M., the officers determined the four-foot grave had three bodies... and began digging with spoons so as not to disturb the grave." So she recreated this scene via a popular Halloween dessert.

This graveyard pudding was served in a rectangular planter to represent the grave itself. In the middle of the pudding were three plastic skeletons to represent the three bodies found. A fake tree branch adorned the top of the pudding which the Johnston Gang used to camouflage the area. A small shovel and spoon were also placed in the pudding. (Author, Bruce Mowday, commented at one of his book talks that he had tasted Cheryl's pudding and "it was his favorite.")

STOTTSVILLE GRAVEYARD PUDDING

1 pkg. (3.4 oz.) instant chocolate pudding mix
12 - 16 oz. dark chocolate cookie crumbs
2 cups cold milk
1 (8 oz.) container whipped topping, thawed
gummy worms

Prepare pudding mix with milk. Let stand for 5 to 10 minutes. Stir in whipped topping and ½ of the cookie crumbs. Top with remaining cookie crumbs. Refrigerate for 1 hour before serving. Decorate with gummy worms.

From The Whine List:

After drinking a glass of *Octorara Red*, someone was heard to have said, "Dad, come get your baby girl. I can't do this job."

NOT SO TASTY

Main Course: *The Particular Sadness of Lemon Cake* by Aimee Bender

Food for Thought:

What does sadness taste like?

Culinary Critique:

Not far into the discussion, it was apparent that the majority of our group did not enjoy this book and said that they would not recommend it to others. As a matter of fact, this was the shortest book discussion that we have had to date. It was almost as if we wanted the discussion to be "over with" so that we could quickly move on to something new. The on-going feeling of the "particular sadness" which started at the beginning of this story was, although touching at times, disturbing and never seemed to end.

On her ninth birthday Rose Edelstein bites into her mother's homemade lemon-chocolate cake and discovers to her surprise and eventual horror that she cannot taste the familiar flavors of lemon or chocolate of one of her favorite desserts. Instead, what she tastes is her mother's emotions *in* the cake. And these emotions are not that of a happy and loving mother and wife, but of hopelessness and distraction. And from that very moment, her every sip, taste and mouthful, are the emotions coming from the person or persons who created whatever fare was presented to her. Needless to say, food, which for all of our club members is something we all love to prepare and share with one another, becomes a curse to Rose for the rest of her life.

This extraordinary tale becomes even more bizarre after we are introduced to Joseph. Joseph is Rose's gifted but troubled brother. By the end of the story, he changes in such a way that it might be incomprehensible to the reader. For Joseph, it was the only way he could cope with the world around him.

Yet, what was interesting about the discussion, even though it was short, was that it was quite energized. And the energy of our discussion was not focused on Rose, the main character, but rather on her mother and father. There seemed to be an almost anger towards these two characters as they did not meet our expectations of how they, as parents, should have been nurturing their highly gifted children. They fostered a dysfunctional family and raised Rose and Joseph to live in what they came to believe was an uncaring and unappreciative world. They deprived their two children from a balance in their life; a balance which can only be attained by love, strength and passion within a family structure which was indeed missing in the Edelstein home.

The OBBC gives *The Particular Sadness of Lemon Cake* **2** spoons out of **5**.

Seasoning: Vice Versa by Sue Young

The Particular Sadness of Lemon Cake was a one of a kind novel with unique ways to look at and talk about food. After discussing the book, we took a verbal trip down memory lane as we shared with one another our first attempt at using that thing called "the kitchen." The favorite first time challenge for most of us was preparing breakfast. Scrambled eggs, French toast as well as "regular" toast provided for the greatest successes, giving us the confidence to try dishes made with more than one or two ingredients. As she graduated to baking, Sue told us of her very first and unique experience at baking cookies.

When I was about nine or ten years old, my childhood friend, Nancy, and I decided to have a bake sale. Prior to our sale, we sent away for a recipe book from the Nestlé's Company. It contained recipes from other lands. We both loved chocolate chip cookies and wanted to make some international types. We decided to make Norwegian Wafers. The recipe for the wafers called for finely chopped semi-sweet chocolate morsels. I remember wondering how we were going to chop the morsels since we were not allowed to use a knife. We didn't want to bother my mother since we wanted to do all of the preparing and baking by ourselves. I got the idea that we should go to the cellar to my father's work bench area and find some tools to finely chop up the chocolate chips. Looking through my father's tools I got the idea that we could put the morsels in a plastic bag and place them in a vice. We thought we had the solution as to how to chop those chocolate chips. OH HOW WRONG WE WERE!

Turning the vice over and over again did not produce chopped morsels. Instead, we were left with one large block of chocolate. What were we going to do next? We used a hammer to break up the block into numerous chunks and then saying to each other, "Guess we will just give up on making the Norwegian Wafers and make chocolate chip cookies from America." After we reduced the chunks to "regular sized morsels," we were set and ready to make the cookie dough and bake. Even though this first experience with baking was a bit upsetting, it did not keep me out of the kitchen. Today, I love to bake!

Side Dish: <u>Entangled</u> by Laurie Cazille

Unlike the majority of OBBC members, one of us loved the book and plans to read it again. She was fascinated by how Rose learned to cope with her "gift" and learned to live with what she could not control. Laurie delighted in the author's descriptive language and untamed imagination.

The Morsel Of The Story

When I read a book and am introduced to a character, setting or object, I like the facts to be presented with the most intimate detail. Afterwards, I decide how much I liked or didn't like the book itself. The author of this book provided me with a new challenge as a reader. She led me down a path of personalities and behaviors that were difficult to grasp. When I reached the end of the story, it was not clear as to what was Bender's purpose and message. Do the actions of a dysfunctional family occur naturally, or are these actions somehow nurtured?

For example, you may find a tree rooted and thriving. Then one day that same tree may be uprooted or have its limbs begin to become entangled and unable to find their way to the sky. Does the entanglement of the branches occur naturally, or does someone or something interfere with its growth? Is this what happened to Rose and Joseph in The Particular Sadness of Lemon Cake? *Are their acquired abnormalities a part of nature, or have they been forced to change because they were manipulated by their environment, or perhaps, by those closest to them, their family? What brings them to the point of so much sadness and despair?*

This story made me realize that there may never be an answer to the lifelong struggles that many people and families face. Not every struggle can be explained as part of living and dying, or can it be healed by love, kindness or compassion. In the case of Rose and Joseph, there was no one to help them survive in their so isolated world.

a la Carte:

Pepperoni Potato Casserole:

Rose discovered that she was able to identify from where many of the foods she ate originated. For example, if she ate a potato, she could identify from which state it was grown. Wanting to add an Italian side dish to the main course using potatoes, a casserole was created with some Italian essentials, pepperoni and mozzarella cheese.

PEPPERONI POTATO CASSEROLE

---

1 pkg. scalloped potatoes
1½ cups water
4 oz. sliced pepperoni
1 can (16 oz.) tomatoes

¼ tsp. oregano leaves
4 oz. shredded mozzarella cheese
4 oz. shredded provolone cheese

In a saucepan, bring tomatoes, water and oregano to a boil; stir in potatoes and packet of seasoning sauce. Pour into an ungreased 1 qt. casserole dish. Arrange pepperoni on top and sprinkle with cheese. Bake uncovered for 30-35 minutes at 400 degrees.

Tumbon - The Pride of the Manetta Family:

When Rose summons up the courage to cook her first meal, it is one of Gina's favorites, spaghetti. Actually, anything pasta is one of her favorites. Growing up, her family always served a special lasagna dish every Christmas and Easter. Unlike traditional lasagna, this dish, called Tumbon, is made with Swiss cheese and mozzarella cheese instead of ricotta. Filled with meat sauce and mushrooms, Tumbon is a hearty and delicious specialty brought over to the U.S. by her grandmother from Abruzzi, Italy.

TUMBON

- 2 lbs. ground beef
- 1 tsp. olive oil
- 1 medium onion, diced
- 2 medium cloves of garlic, peeled and minced
- 2 lbs. mushrooms
- 2 (15 oz.) cans tomato sauce
- 1 Tbs. tomato paste
- ½ tsp. dried oregano, crushed
- 16 lasagna noodles
- 2 cups coarsely grated mozzarella cheese
- 1 cup coarsely grated Swiss cheese
- ½ cup parmesan cheese
- salt and pepper to taste

In a large heavy skillet, brown the ground beef. Drain well, transfer to a container and set aside. In same skillet, heat olive oil at medium setting adding onion and garlic. Sauté for 5 minutes. Return cooked ground beef to the skillet adding tomato sauce, paste and oregano. Bring to a boil. Reduce heat and simmer for 30 minutes. Set aside. Cook the noodles according to the package directions. Drain and spread out onto a kitchen towel. Spread a thin layer of the meat sauce over the bottom of a 9 X 13-inch baking dish. Top with a layer of noodles running down the length of the dish. Spread ⅓ of the meat sauce over noodles, followed by a layer of mushrooms and a layer of mozzarella and Swiss cheeses. Cover with second layer of noodles running crosswise, ⅓ of the meat sauce and the remaining mushrooms and cheese. Again cover the remaining noodles running the length of the dish, top with remaining sauce and sprinkle with the parmesan cheese. Bake Tumbon in a preheated 350 degree oven for 40 minutes. Let dish stand for 10 minutes before serving.

Chair Man's Lemon Trifle:

This recipe was named for both the reference in the title to lemon cake and for the outcome of one of the characters at the end of the story.

CHAIR MAN'S LEMON TRIFLE

8 oz. container of Cool Whip
2 pkgs. prepared lemon pudding

lemon pound cake (cut into bite size pieces)
lemon slices for garnish

Simply layer all ingredients – cake, pudding, cool whip making 2 layers and garnish with lemon slices.

From The Whine List:

After drinking a glass of *Cupcake Malbec,* someone was heard to have said, "Mom liked the boys best."

A PICTURE IS WORTH A THOUSAND WORDS

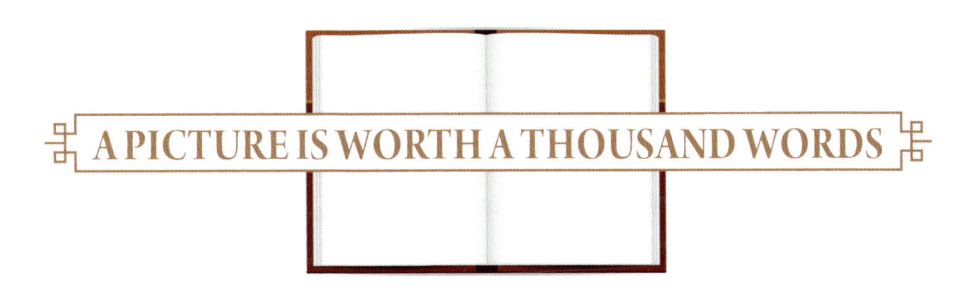

Main Course: *The Girl with the Dragon Tattoo* by Stieg Larsson

Food for Thought:

Everyone has at least one guilty pleasure!

Culinary Critique:

This exciting introduction to "The Girl" Trilogy by Steig Larsson had a little something unexpected for each of the members of our book club. Mysterious exotic flowers, dark family secrets, hostile company takeovers, sex and violence, all came together to keep our brains spinning, and at times, out of control.

To get to the main part of the story, we needed to "plow through" many names of people and places in a language with which we were not familiar. And, setting up to read a trilogy made it necessary to read through a lot of background information about not only the Vanger family, but also the many other characters whose lives would have a profound impact on the overall plot. Keeping track of all of this information of facts, figures, names and places in Svenska, as Swedes call their language, was challenging at best. But the learning of new words and names of new places was well worth it, as we were led through an exciting search of a young heiress to one of the wealthiest families in Sweden, forty years after her disappearance. Had she been murdered, did she die in a tragic accident or was she still alive?

The Morsel Of The Story

Determined to solve this mystery is Mikael Blomkvist, a distinguished and experienced forty-eight year old journalist who is introduced to a twenty-four year old pierced and tattooed computer hacker, Lisbeth Salander. Together, this very unlikely duo discovers the evil and corruption behind the Vanger family which may have led to the disappearance of the young scion to the Vanger estate.

Our overall fascination with this novel was not the overall plot, as much as it was with one of the main characters, Lisbeth Salander. Everything about her was intense and extreme from her outward appearance to her mental perceptions, not to mention her lifestyle. We were quite intrigued by her free will and even applauded some the choices she made. Having been a victim of abuse all of her life, Lisbeth demonstrated a deep courage which made her, in our eyes, a heroine for all women who had been physically or mentally abused. Despite many of her unorthodox ways of finding solutions to problems, this character demonstrated how one can survive after having been pushed to one's emotional limit.

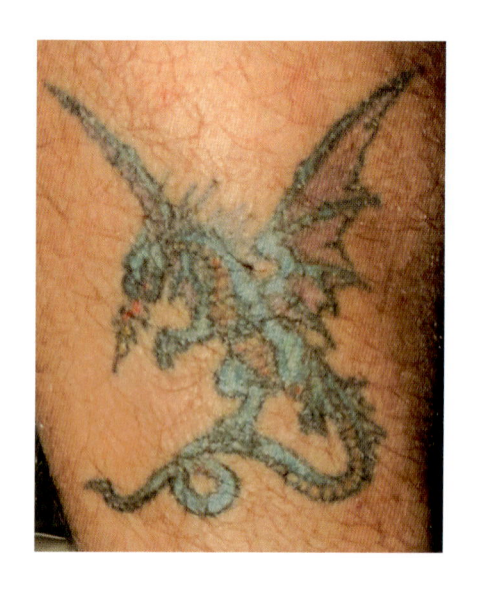

The Girl with the Dragon Tattoo is indeed an intriguing mystery, but, our recommendation would be that as a "stand alone" it leaves the reader needing more. The ending is like falling off a cliff and not knowing if you survived the fall. So, be prepared for the reading of three books, not just one.

The OBBC gives *The Girl With The Dragon Tattoo* **3** spoons 🥄🥄🥄 out of **5**.

Seasoning: Popcorn, Anyone? by Cheryl Proudfoot

It has been said that "the movie was not as good as the book." In many cases, this is indeed true. We have all rushed to the movie theater in anticipation of seeing if the visions presented by an author matched those of the screen writer and/or the movie director. Nevertheless, the details provided by the movie script and visual images from *The Girl With The Dragon Tattoo* did not disappoint.

It is not often that we find a movie which matches our imagination as readers, but, there are a few. Here are our picks!

The Godfather by Mario Puzo, 1969

The Exorcist by William Peter Blatty, 1971

The Shining by Stephen King, 1978

Side Dish: Stigma by Gina Hove

There is an old American Proverb that I learned in school, "don't judge a book by its cover," a metaphorical phrase meaning you should not prejudge the worth of someone or something solely by an outward appearance. But that is exactly what I did before opening to the first page of the novel, The Girl With The Dragon Tattoo. I conjured up a vision of not only a colorful dragon adorning the leg, neck, ankle, hand or some other part of a young girl's body, but of a girl who by the standards of long ago was rebellious and irresponsible . When I was growing up, people were harshly judged by the way they dressed and by their overall looks and mannerisms. Unlike today, there was a great deal of stereotyping surrounding men and women with tattoos. In this day and age, tattoos are much more accepted and have become quite popular.

The Morsel Of The Story

I, myself, do not have a tattoo, but the reading of this novel brought back a memory of accompanying a friend "Jane," as she set out to get her first one, as well as my own negative preconceived notions with which I had been brought up. It was a summer day in the late 1970's when Jane surprised me with her decision to get a tattoo. And before I could talk her out of it, she said, "My mind is made up and I am going to have it done today." I agreed to accompany her, hoping that during the drive to our destination I would be able to change her mind. During the drive to a town two hours away (not wanting to risk running into anyone we knew), I tried to convince her that tattoos were not for upstanding young women but reserved for someone who spent time in prison or was part of a motorcycle gang. (Boy, how times have changed.)

Finding the address someone had written for her on a torn piece of paper, she and I entered a small (very small) shop; more like a big room. Our entrance was made known by the tinkling of a bell atop the door of the shop. The lighting inside was quite dim which I found odd since I thought that lighting would be an important component for this type of work. In the middle of the room was a chair, much like that of a dentist chair. And next to the chair was a table with what looked like a dentist's drill and different pots of colored ink.

Emerging from the back of the shop came a rather large man, dressed in blue jeans, a t-shirt and a black leather vest; the artist. My body language began screaming, "maybe we should go." But either my friend did not hear me or was not listening. Instead, she quickly moved to a wall of "artwork" and was busy making her selection. She, then, hopped into the "dentist" chair. After describing the colors for her tattoo and identifying a discreet location to where to paint her masterpiece, the artist began painting the most delicate butterfly to become part of my friend's personal landscape. And after about two hours of his drilling, the continual wiping of blood from the "drilled" area so that he could see his work more clearly, and MY perfuse sweating, the work was completed and we were on our way home.

During the trip home I again began thinking about that old American Proverb. I couldn't help but think that Jane would now be forever perceived as either a criminal, drug addict or worse. But Jane was not thinking of that proverb at all. She was thinking more like Ralph Waldo Emerson. She was not worried about someone prejudging her by her appearance. She was feeling satisfied and confident that she was expressing her individuality and "marching to the beat of her own drum."

a la Carte:

Tatted-Up Coffee:

Boiled coffee was a staple beverage referred to in the book. Rather than using a modern day coffee urn, we made boiled coffee in a pan and served it with heavy cream. It earned its name from the title, "tattoo."

TATTED-UP COFFEE

2 oz. spice flavored coffee
whipped cream
water (enough to make 8 to 10 cups)

Bring water to a rapid boil then pour over coffee grounds. Use a strainer lined with a paper towel over a standard sauce pan. Return the pan to the stove and use medium heat to create a strong aroma while the coffee maintains heat. Pour into mugs or cups and top with whipped cream.

Elsie's Luncheonette:

To go with our coffee, Laurie made a number of different types of sandwiches. Coffee and sandwiches were an often mentioned combination throughout the book. Served on deli sliced bread, these sandwiches of ham, egg and chicken salad make a great meal or snack for any occasion. And, if you are looking to add something different to this tray of traditional tea sandwiches, try an Onion on Rye. Laurie learned to make all of these sandwiches from her mother, Elsie, in their busy kitchen on Black Horse Hill in Coatesville, Pa. Friends and family were always coming in and out that it often felt like a diner or luncheonette.

ONION ON RYE

½ of rye bread or small tea sandwich loaf
2 large yellow onions, cut finely
1 cup mayonnaise
1 cup parmesan cheese
salt and pepper to taste

Cut bread into half pieces and make one flat layer on a baking sheet. Mix onion, mayonnaise, parmesan cheese, salt and pepper together. Place mixture on top of bread layer, about 1 Tbs. on each slice. Bake at 350 degrees for about 10 minutes until light brown.

CHICKEN SALAD

4 cooked boneless chicken breast

1 green pepper

1 cup mayonnaise

Shred chicken into small pieces. Dice pepper and mix with chicken. Add salt and pepper to taste. Mix in mayonnaise. Refrigerate until serving. Spread on bread or rolls.

HAM SALAD

2 cups fresh minced ham

1 small onion

½ jar relish (Indian)

¼ - ½ cup mayonnaise

pepper

Grind ham and onion together. Add relish, pepper to taste and enough mayonnaise to your liking. Great served with crackers or bread.

EGG SALAD

6 hard boiled eggs

2 tsp. relish or chopped butter pickles

⅛ cup mayonnaise

salt and pepper to taste

Cut up eggs. Add relish or chopped butter pickles and salt and pepper to taste. Mix in mayonnaise to desired consistency. Place on bread and cut into 4 pieces for tea sandwiches.

From The Whine List:

After drinking a glass of *Cardinal Zin*, someone was heard to have said, "I'll do anything on my death bed."

IMAGINE

Main Course: *The Shack* by William Young

Food for Thought:

Face - to - Face

Culinary Critique:

Two separate opinions defined our reaction to the believability of the reality of mortal man interacting directly with the Holy Trinity in a mountain shack in the state of Oregon. Half of the group believed that it was possible for Mackenzie Phillips to have had an encounter with God. The other half thought his experience must have been the result of a dream or a hallucination. Regardless of whether or not the days that Mackenzie Phillips spent with God were authentic or imagined, we were left with a stronger sense of the love and forgiveness of our Creator; a God who is always with us and will never abandon us.

Our book club is represented by different branches of Christianity. Whether Protestant or Catholic, we all agreed that *"Papa"* wants to share with us the "joy and freedom and light of his love." We were created to be in a "face-to-face relationship" joined together with The Father, The Son and The Holy Spirit in "their circle of love."

We tried to put ourselves in the shoes of the main character to see where God would have invited *us* to meet him. Many members shared very personal stories of their toughest trials and deepest pains and how they wished there would have been a "shack" for them, where they could have better understood and in turn dealt with His purpose and plan.

All felt inspired to take the book's main message, the gift of forgiveness, and use it more fervently in their future lives. Some even were so inspired by Mack's encounter with God that their acts of forgiveness were set in motion even before the book club meeting was ever called to order. "Forgive those who have offended you; not for them, but for yourself." (Harriet Nelson)

The OBBC gives *The Shack* **5** spoons 🥄🥄🥄🥄🥄 out of **5**.

Seasoning: Summing It Up by Donna McElwee

In *The Shack,* Young challenges the reader to think about his/her relationship with God. We believe that Donna best summed up our thoughts and feelings. She writes:

God has always been an integral part of my life. I pray to God every day. I pray to Him for my loved ones as well as for the sick and the oppressed as I hope they pray for me. I was always told that God is everywhere and that He is a part of everything; I believe this. God is my sunshine and my rain, my good and my bad, my happy and my sad and I know He is always with me.

Side Dish: Thank You by Gina Hove

I was brought up in a strict Catholic-Italian environment which provided for me a very strong background in my faith. This upbringing was not so strict that is caused a fear of the church, but a sense of consistency and understanding of what my parents said would make me a good Catholic; Mass on Sunday, weekly novenas, monthly confessions and saying the Rosary.

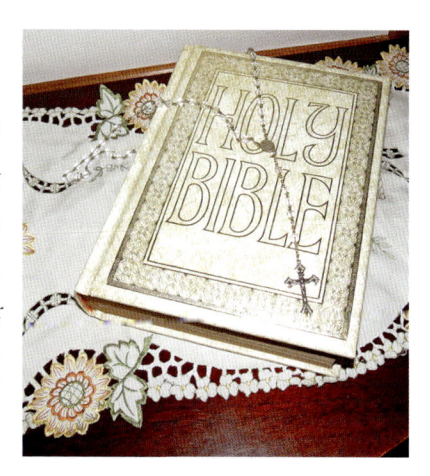

From 1958 through 1967, I was enrolled in St. Cecilia Catholic School in Coatesville, Pa. I have very fond memories of those days and loved the nuns. Like many of the rest of my elementary school girlfriends, I was going to be a nun. Once a week, my very best friend, Mary Beth, and I played out our fantasies by volunteering to help the nuns at the convent with the cleaning of the chapel, and going with them downtown to help with the shopping. When our work was done, we were sometimes asked to join "the sisters" at the kitchen table for a bowl of ice cream. (Who would have thought their favorite flavor was spumoni.)

Neither I, or any of my classmates, entered the convent but we still have many fond and funny memories of our Catholic school education. Today when we get together we usually end up sharing some of our favorite stories, including the ones that everyone has heard about, i.e. sitting straight with our hands folded on the top of our desks, the uniforms, pagan babies, the "ruler," the sin of wearing black patent leather shoes and Mother Superior's "clicker."

Fast forward to 1971. I attended West Chester State College, (now known as West Chester University). This was my first experience away from home. It was during my college days that I became very lukewarm about my faith. I stopped going to Mass and novena, and saying the rosary. I still believed in God, and I went to Mass on the "important" days, like

Christmas and Easter. Before I knew it, I had graduated from WCSC, earned a number of degrees, advanced through my career and was married, but just became too busy for God. Like Mackenzie in The Shack, *I had lost my relationship with God. I had a lot of time and energy for everyone else, but no time for God.*

Fast forward again to the summer of 2008. I guess God had had enough of my lukewarm approach to my faith and presented me with a tragedy. On the morning of August 6, my mother was experiencing chest pains and was rushed to the hospital. Over the course of the next seven hours, my mother's heart had stopped beating three times. And each time that her heart stopped beating, I fell to my knees and prayed for the intercession of God and The Blessed Mother and all the angels and saints. And it was indeed the power of prayer that started her heart to beat each time it had stopped. Her doctors shook their heads and couldn't understand or explain what happened that day. Her chief cardiologist, taking no credit for my mother's recovery said, "We may have kept her afloat, but it was God who pulled her out of the water." We both knew what really did happen was a miracle. Much like Mackenzie in The Shack, *we learned that it is God who has the supreme power over all. And just like Mack, my life was forever changed by the gift of a wonderful miracle.*

I started getting back to my old roots, dusted off my rosaries and reacquainted myself with those truths which had guided me in the early days of my youth. The first steps to return to the tenants of the Catholic Church and traditional observances were easy. Going to Mass regularly as well as devoting myself more deeply to prayer quickly became a joyful daily practice. But... going back to "confession" was not going to be easy. God was trying to bring me back into grace and to get there, I was going to have to receive the sacraments, not on my terms, but on His.

Confession. As a catholic, I was going to have to tell a priest that I had not been to confession for 37 years AND unlike the confessionals of my youth, I couldn't "hide" behind a screen; there would be no anonymity. I discovered that the "set-up" for the confessional, since I had last attended, had changed. I would have to meet my confessor face to face. The very thought of returning to the confessional booth filled me with anxiety and dread.

After much apprehension, I built up my courage, and on Saturday, June 13, 2009, I headed for St. Cecilia's Church, the church of my "old" elementary school; the church where I first received the Sacrament of Reconciliation. Driving to the church I practiced by reciting the familiar phrase, "Bless me Father, for I have sinned," listed my offenses and the number of times I had committed them. I prepared myself for a lecture from the priest and I saw myself leaving the confessional to recite more than just a few" Hail Mary's " and "Our Father's."

I arrived 20 minutes before the designated time for confession to begin and was the first in line. I prayed and stared at the confessional waiting for the little red lamp above the door of the confessional to light indicating that the priest was ready. After what seemed to be an eternity, the light finally went on. I took a deep breath and made my way to the confessional, opened the door and entered to find a small room with two chairs. In one of the chairs sat the priest who greeted me with a gentle and welcoming smile. After explaining that I had been away so long, he said, "Don't worry trying to remember and list all of your sins. Just being here, God will know your sins and will forgive you. For your penance, go home and before you go to bed tonight, tell God 'thank you'."

Maria, Gina and Laurie at the Vatican

a la Carte:

R & C Seafood Chowder:

The mention of Papa's clam chowder prompted Cheryl L. and Rick to prepare a wonderful white fish seafood chowder. So, in recognition of these two fantastic "chefs" we named this dish for R (Rick) and C (Cheryl).

R + C SEAFOOD CHOWDER

- 1 cup each chopped onion, carrot and celery
- 8 Tbs. butter
- ½ lb. small cooked shrimp
- ½ lb. sea scallops, diced
- 1 lb. mild white fish (haddock, cod) cut into 1 inch chunks
- 3 - 5 medium potatoes, diced
- 3 (8 oz. bottles) clam juice

- 2 cups chicken broth
- 1½ cups water
- 2 cups light cream
- 1 cup milk
- 1 tsp. Old Bay
- 2 Tbs. fresh parsley
- 3 heaping Tbs. flour or corn starch
- salt and pepper to taste

Melt 5 Tbs. butter in pan. Add onion, celery, parsley and carrot. Sauté until vegetables are tender. Add potatoes, 1 cup of water, chicken broth and clam juice. Cover and boil approximately 20 minutes until potatoes are soft. Heat milk and cream in small saucepan until warm. Add to mixture along with seasonings and remaining 3 Tbs. butter. Add shrimp and scallops. Fold in white fish. Bring to low boil, reduce heat and simmer for 15 minutes. In separate container, mix approximately 3 Tbs. flour or corn starch to ½ cup water to make thickening. Add thickening to chowder for desired consistency.

Sacred Triple Chocolate Brownies:

Also included in this meal around the camp fire were brownies. Cheryl P. made a special brownie to enjoy as we discussed this book. What better way to perfect the brownie than to add three kinds of chocolate.

SACRED TRIPLE CHOCOLATE BROWNIES

3 sq. (3 oz.) Hershey's semi-sweet baking chocolate

½ cup butter or margarine

1 cup sugar

2 eggs

½ cup sifted flour

¾ tsp. vanilla

⅛ cup each semi-sweet and milk chocolate morsels

¾ cup coarsely chopped walnuts (optional)

Preheat oven to 350 degrees. Grease 8 inch square pan. Melt chocolate (leave in wrappers while melting) in double boiler. Cream butter and sugar together. Add unbeaten eggs, one at a time. Add flour and mix thoroughly. Stir in melted chocolate, vanilla, chocolate chips and nuts (optional) and pour into pan. Bake 25 to 30 minutes – no longer. Brownie tops should still be rather soft when touched with finger. Cool in pan and cut in squares.

Melt In Your Mouth Scones:

At the cabin house, scones appeared for breakfast by what Mack would identify as divine intervention. Our positively divine Melt in Your Mouth Scones can easily be made by preparing your favorite scone recipe and adding lots of chocolate chips (or any other favorite "morsels" i.e. cranberries, walnuts, etc.).

MELT IN YOUR MOUTH SCONES

- 2 cups Bisquick
- ½ cup chocolate chip morsels
- ⅓ cup low-fat milk
- 3 Tbs. sugar
- 1 tsp. vanilla
- 1 egg
- crushed pecans (optional)

Mix together all ingredients except the pecans. Form into an 8 inch circle. Use more Bisquick if this is sticky. Brush with milk and sprinkle with sugar. Put on greased cookie sheet. Cut into eighths before baking. Bake at 425 degrees for 12 minutes.

From The Whine List:

After drinking a glass of *St. Francis Old Vines Zinfandel*, someone was heard to have said, "Lord, keep your arm around my shoulder and your hand over my mouth."

SELF-DISCOVERY

Main Dish: *Home Safe* by Elizabeth Berg

Food for Thought:

Just when you thought it was safe…

Culinary Critique:

Helen Ames, a popular modern day author, goes through a period of writer's block, following the death of her husband. Looking for inspiration to help her get back to writing again, she decides to take the job as the teacher of a writing class. This new experience leads her to self-discovery, changing the way she views herself and others. By teaching others to believe in their own work and abilities, she is able to gain back her own confidence.

Home Safe was one of our favorite books. Each OBBC member found it easy to relate to Helen Ames, particularly in the way she learned how to work through her problems. After being faced with an unforeseen tragedy she finds a way to persevere and evolve into a stronger woman.

The life of Helen Ames, with her husband Dan, and daughter, Tessa, was basically and fundamentally a good life. Through many examples, Berg gives us a look into the life of an almost perfect family. One example occurs when Dan surprises Helen with a gift of a special house which could only have been imagined by a man totally in tune with his wife's deepest desires and dreams. Another is seen when Helen's daughter Tessa, getting ready to leave home to start her own life, creates a personally designed "test" that Helen must take to convince Tessa that she will be safe after her daughter has moved away. These are just two examples that demonstrated to us that when we put the needs of others above our own, we can only be left with complete love and happiness.

One other important message marked by Berg in *Home Safe* was the message of simplicity. This is played out with the description of Helen's beautiful family tradition of placing a wrapped empty box each year under the Christmas tree. What can an empty box teach us? A simple truth. No matter what you think you may need to better your life, first consider what you already have.

The OBBC gives *Home Safe* **5** spoons 🥄🥄🥄🥄🥄 out of **5**.

Seasoning: Difficult by Euna Scott

Helen Ames, in her role as writing teacher, taught her students that writing about personal experiences would help them become good writers.

At the meeting when we discussed this novel, Laurie took on the role of Helen, "the writing teacher." She assigned to each of us a topic which became a homework assignment to be prepared for the next meeting. The essay below was written by Euna. Her essay could very well have been written by Helen as it represented "The Most Difficult Situation of My Life."

The most difficult situation that I had to face was that of the death of my husband. He had been retired for several years due to disability and wanted me to retire with him so that we could take a month long vacation out West. While planning our trip, he developed an aneurysm and had to have surgery. Before he left for the hospital, he told me, "in case I don't come home, check on top of the kitchen cupboard."

He never regained consciousness from that operation when he was transferred to another hospital for bypass surgery. Both operations were successful. But after a few weeks, I received a phone call from the hospital telling me that my dear husband had died. I, at that time, felt unprepared; so much to do, so little time.

Many months after John passed away, I remembered what he told me about checking the kitchen cupboard. Standing on a chair so that I could reach to the top of the cupboard, I discovered an old glass pickle jar. Inside and wrapped in aluminum foil were five - one hundred dollar bills. He must have known how unprepared I would be. I kept those one hundred dollar bills wrapped in foil and it makes me smile. Understand, my husband was a farmer. Money was always tight. I know how difficult it must have been to save that mere pittance. But save he did to protect our love and our family.

Side Dish: <u>Moving On</u> by Cheryl Laurento

It was my father's dream for me to become a nurse. I was accepted into nursing school but my heart was not in it. Although it would disappoint my father, I changed my plans. Instead of going to school I married my high school sweetheart, gave birth to a child, then divorced a few years later. I was 22 years old.

Over time I had a number of different jobs. While rearing my son, I worked in the collections department of a bank, as a clerk in a paint factory and as a waitress in several different restaurants. After meeting difficulties that I couldn't manage on my own, I moved back with my parents at age 25. So much for living the dream, my father's or mine.

One night I ran into a guy who recognized me from my childhood days when we lived a few doors from each other. He was eight years older than me so I really didn't remember Larry as well as some of his siblings. He said I threw sticks at him because he wouldn't let me play basketball. Who knew that would be a memorable occasion for him. Of course, he could have made that up.

He would try anything to get me to notice him. One night I remember having to take him home after he told me his friend had stranded him. I later found out that he wasn't left stranded after all. He had arranged for his friend to leave without him so that he could spend time with me. He was a con artist after all.

I tried to ignore his advances as long as I could. When he would call me on the phone to ask me out, I would tell him I was in love with someone else. But, he was very persistent. One night he called me and asked me to come to a party because his friends had surprised him with a birthday cake. That was the night that I realized that I really did care for him. We were engaged the following year and married exactly one year from the day we got engaged.

Till death do us part… and so it was. Eight years of marriage, ups and downs, his three children and my one all sharing fun times and laughter. Then it happened. The one thing no one expects, the life-changing event. He was diagnosed with a brain tumor. I never gave up hope, or maybe I just couldn't face the inevitable. After a year and a half of working all day and spending every evening beside him at the hospital, he was gone. No more hospital visits. How do I fill this void? How long until the tears and longing end? And I don't feel this hole in my heart? I didn't have an answer. I just knew that I was at that proverbial Y in the road where I made the decision to move on and try to make life better for the kids. They were all teenagers with many milestones ahead of them that their father would not be able to share. And at each of those occasions we would all feel his absence.

During Larry's hospitalization I spent many hours witnessing the interventions that the medical personnel performed, making judgments about their caring demeanors, or lack

Self-Discovery

thereof, and feeling that I could be the caregiver that every patient deserved. So I did move forward and decided to go to nursing school.

It was a slow transition from the mourning widow to the determined student. One step at a time, one foot in front of the other. My father died before my graduation, but he died knowing that his daughter was finally fulfilling not only his dream but that of her own. So from the depths of sorry for the loss of the man I loved came the crossroad. I took the high road in his honor.

a la Carte:

James' Special Slaw:

Donetta describes the kitchen as a room of great meaning. James (her husband) liked to make coleslaw. He would eat it every day if you let him. The recipe died with him. The only ingredient that Donetta knew was barbecue sauce.

Laurie thought she would give this a try and added barbecue sauce to her mother's coleslaw recipe. Our first reaction was, "Coleslaw with barbecue sauce?" But, all it took was one taste and we were hooked. You will be too!

JAMES' SPECIAL SLAW

1 head of cabbage
2 - 3 carrots
1 cup mayonnaise
½ cup sugar
1 tsp. vinegar

½ cup catsup
6 drops Worcestershire sauce
¼ cup brown sugar
Shred cabbage into a fine slaw along with carrots.

Dressing - Mix mayonnaise, vinegar and sugar. Whisk until mixture turns a yellow color. The taste should be sweet with a hint of vinegar. Refrigerate.

Barbecue sauce – Mix catsup, Worcestershire sauce and brown sugar. Whisk and do another taste test for both sweet and sour. Refrigerate.

When ready to serve, mix cabbage with the coleslaw dressing making sure the consistency is not too moist. Add barbecue sauce to change color and taste. This is an old family recipe that the ingredients were never measured out. So by trial and error, one can judge for taste and consistency.

English Toast Casserole:

In this story, Helen taught her daughter how to make French toast. Deb decided she would prepare for us her family's French toast casserole which she makes every Christmas. We renamed it English Toast Casserole because the heroine of the story was a teacher of writing, who in our high school days used to be called our *English* teacher.

ENGLISH TOAST CASSEROLE

1 loaf raisin bread, cubed
6 eggs, lightly beaten
1½ cups milk
½ cup half & half
1 tsp. cinnamon
¼ cup butter, sliced

½ tsp. vanilla
¼ tsp. salt
¼ cup toasted pecans, chopped
⅓ cup brown sugar
maple syrup

This recipe should be prepared the night before or at least 3 - 4 hours before baking. In a medium bowl, mix milk, half & half, salt, eggs and vanilla until lightly beaten. Using a deep 8 X 8 inch baking pan, layer half of the raisin bread cubes. Pour half of egg/milk mixture on top. Top with slivers of butter (only half the amount of butter). Layer in the rest of the bread cubes and pour the remaining mixture on top. Evenly sprinkle brown sugar over casserole then finish off the rest of the slivered butter. Top off the casserole with toasted pecans. Cover casserole with plastic wrap and refrigerate overnight or if baking same day, let casserole soak for 3 - 4 hours inside refrigerator. When ready, bake at 350 degrees for 45-50 minutes. Casserole should look puffy and golden brown on top when done. Serve with maple syrup.

Drive Thru Lemon Sponge Pie:

Sue decided to treat us to her very first attempt at making a lemon sponge pie. She also loved the idea of the playhouse take-out window and thus named her dessert Drive Thru Lemon Sponge Pie. It baked up perfectly. You would have thought that she had made it many times before.

DRIVE THRU LEMON SPONGE PIE

1 unbaked pie shell
2 Tbs. butter
1 cup sugar
2⅛ Tbs. flour

juice + grated rind of 1 lemon
1⅛ cups milk
3 eggs

Cream butter, sugar, flour and yolks of 3 eggs together. Add lemon juice and rind. Stir well. Add milk. Beat egg whites until stiff and add to mixture. Pour into pie shell and bake at 375 degrees for 20-25 minutes.

Backup Apple Crisp:

(Sue confessed that if the lemon sponge pie "flopped," she would have a "back-up.")

BACKUP APPLE CRISP
---

4 cups of sliced McIntosh apples
1 tsp. cinnamon
½ tsp. salt
¼ cup water

¾ cup sifted flour
½ cup sugar
½ cup butter

Place apples in greased 10 X 6 X 2 inch baking dish. Sprinkle with cinnamon, salt and water. Rub together flour, sugar and butter. Drop crumbled mixture over apples. Bake at 350 degrees for 40 minutes.

From The Whine List:

After drinking a glass of *Smart Cookie Sauvignon Blanc,* someone was heard to have said: "She made dessert?; **she never** makes dessert." Then we heard, "I didn't say it was a good dessert; I just said I made dessert."

TRAPPED

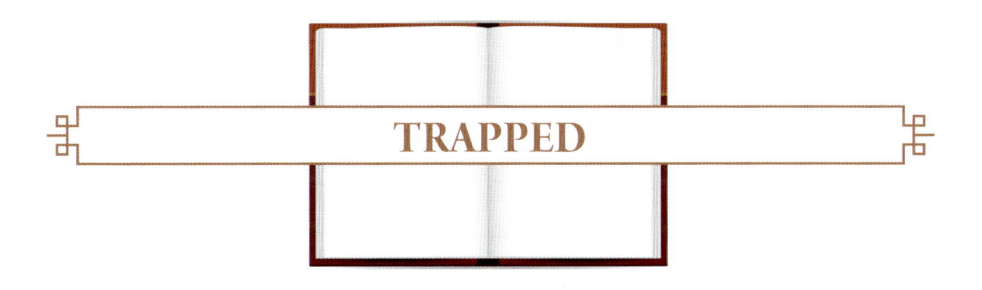

Main Course: *The Yellow Wallpaper* by Charlotte Perkins Gilman

Food for Thought:

If the walls in your house could talk, what would they say?

Culinary Critique:

The Yellow Wallpaper is the personal account of a woman, known only as the narrator, who is diagnosed with hysteria and whose cure leads her to madness. Although a work of fiction, this short story is an exaggerated version of the author's own experiences with depression. In real life, Gilman's physician diagnosed her with neurasthenia, later to be known as "hysteria," a feminine disorder of the late 1880's. Her treatment, as was presented in the story, was complete rest. Gilman projected this on to her main character who was not allowed to read or write, or care for her newborn baby.

The narrator of the story was not permitted to be in her own home and was taken to a new location in a country house, where she felt imprisoned, unable to do anything except remain in a room to ponder the "hypnotic patterns of the faded yellow wallpaper." Over time she began to imagine women trapped in the wallpaper. There was one woman in particular that she set out to free and capture. But why this one woman over the others? As we discover by the end of the tale, our narrator is totally insane and she herself is the woman in the wallpaper whom she desperately tries to free.

We felt pity for this character and were all in agreement that she was suffering from more than just "hysteria." For her to be in such a mental state which would leave her to imagine eyes peering out from a wall, indicated a serious case of some type of mental disorder. She was tragically misdiagnosed.

Considered a first wave feminist, Gilman presents a second theme, the role of women at the end of the nineteenth century. The superiority of men over women is made clear by the description of her husband, John, and his overall authoritative behavior towards her. The narrator of the story lives in a society where women are not to voice their opinions or stand up to their husbands. John patronizes and dominates his wife all in the name of "curing" her. He treats her more like a child than a wife referring to her as his "precious little goose." He never calls her by name. We were quite amused at the turn of events in the closing scene of the story, visualizing an insane woman "creeping" over her fainted husband and in the end becoming the dominant figure.

The reading of this short story led us to suppose what would cause a woman of the 21st Century to fall into "hysteria." We considered the gamut of modern day scenarios which might have given our narrator cause for her nervous breakdown. Possibilities included postpartum depression, brain illness, schizophrenia, the loss of a child and a husband's plot against his wife for the love of another woman. It was quite the imaginative discussion.

The OBBC gives *The Yellow Wallpaper* **3** spoons out of **5**.

Seasoning: <u>If the Walls Could Talk</u> by Deb Patton

When we arrived at our book club meeting for the discussion of *The Yellow Wallpaper*, we found that the hostess had decorated her home to recreate the second floor nursery room of the mansion to where the heroine of the story had been banished. We immediately began to describe the "women" whose eyes were peering at us through "the wallpaper" by giving them a voice. We imagined that the ladies trapped in the wallpaper represented the feelings of women at the turn of the nineteenth century and the patriarchal oppression that they were forced to endure. This is what we heard:

> *"I am a loving mother, a faithful partner, a loyal friend and a devoted child. I struggle to find time for all of my loved ones. I struggle to find time for me."*
>
> *"My life has become meaningless."*
>
> *"I am disenchanted with society and the state of the world."*
>
> *"I am disappointed with how people treat one another. I am frustrated by how women are treated."*
>
> *"I am saddened to the point I want to shut myself off so I don't have to face the world."*
>
> *"The responsibilities of work and family cause me to be discontented and bored with life."*
>
> *"How can I escape my discontentment?"*
>
> *"I need to escape from all of my emotions."*

Side Dish: Underneath the Layers by Sue Young

Have you ever tried to remove old wallpaper? Not easy, is it? Back in the 1950's, it was applied with a paste or glue, and was very difficult to remove. When my husband and I moved into our first house, there were several rooms that needed "freshened up" with either a coat of paint or new wallpaper. It was going to be a big job so I decided to start with the kitchen. These walls were covered with an avocado green printed paper which was typically seen in the 1970's. I can remember mixing up a solution of hot water and vinegar and sponging it on the wallpaper. After waiting for the solution to work, I scraped the walls with a metal putty knife. What a mess it made and the smell was horrible! By the time I was done, my clothes were drenched with the vinegar water and I was covered with peels of the old wallpaper. This procedure does not always work the first time. But after more soaking and scraping, I was finally able to remove it. To my surprise, there was another layer of paper under the green printed one. This one was a very old yellowed, stained floral print with bold vertical stripes.

Sitting back looking at the walls, disgusted, resting and trying to gear up to do this job all over again, I began to wonder who lived here before us. How many families shared this home throughout the years? I thought there must have been children living in this house as I found crayon marks on the first paper I had removed. I began to imagine what their life was like. What did they talk about during the many meals they shared in this kitchen?

I imagined lots of great food, lots of laughter, happiness and love, just as it would be for my new family. If only the walls in this old house could talk! They would be able to tell me about some of the people who lived here and the happy events in their lives; and maybe some sad ones too.

After much wondering, I went back to work, finished removing the old paper and got ready for the next day to apply a fresh coat of paint. When the hard work of remodeling and painting of the other rooms was completed, that kitchen by far was my favorite room in that old house.

a la Carte:

All recipes prepared for the discussion of the reading of *The Yellow Wallpaper*, needed to be similar to, but not completely, a "repellent, almost revolting, smoldering yellow." So we started our conversation with an appetizer, (Insane Artichoke Dip), which led into a delicious main course of lemon chicken, (Mellow Yellow Chicken & Squash), ending with a sweet dessert salad (Twisted Pretzel Pineapple Salad).

INSANE ARTICHOKE DIP

1 can artichoke hearts (not marinated)
¼ lb. grated or shredded mozzarella cheese
¾ cup grated parmesan cheese

½ cup shredded six cheese Italian blend
1 cup mayonnaise
crackers of your choice

Drain and mash artichokes. Combine other ingredients and bake at 350 degrees for 20 minutes in a 9 inch pie plate. Use broiler to lightly brown. Serve with crackers. Reheat in microwave.

MELLOW YELLOW CHICKEN & SQUASH

1 lemon (zest and juice)
2 yellow onions, chopped
1 small yellow squash (½ inch slices)
3 lb. chicken (cut to bite size pieces)
1 lb. pasta – any

2 cups chicken broth
2 Tbs. corn starch
2 Tbs. lemon pepper seasoning
1 Tbs. olive oil

Cook pasta in large pot according to the directions. In large skillet, cook onion in olive oil for 3 minutes. Add squash and cook until tender. Add chicken and cook until brown. Thicken chicken broth with cornstarch in a separate saucepan. Add to the ingredients in skillet. Add lemon pepper, lemon juice and zest. Mix and simmer on low heat. Add pasta. Mix well and serve.

TWISTED PRETZEL PINEAPPLE SALAD

2 cups crushed pretzels
1 stick of butter or margarine
½ cup sugar
1 (20 oz.) can of crushed pineapple

2 Tbs. corn starch
1 (8 oz.) container of whipped topped (thawed)
8 oz. softened cream cheese

Mix pretzels and ¼ cup of sugar. Melt butter or margarine and add to pretzels. Press into a 13 X 9 pan. Bake for 8 minutes at 400 degrees. Cool. Mix crushed pineapple and corn starch and cook in a medium saucepan until thick. Cool. Blend together whipped topping, cream cheese and ¼ cup of sugar. Spread on baked pretzel crust. Top with pineapple mixture. Refrigerate. Cut and enjoy!

From The Whine List:

After drinking a glass of *Running With Scissors Cabernet,* someone was heard to have said, "Monday my life will be normal."

Pièce de Résistance

The Best Part!

We all listened intently, young and old.

SMARTY PANTS

One of the members suggested we read a children's' book. No, not for the large print or for the colorful pictures, but because of the wonderful way children's' books present answers to many of life's questions.

In this charming story about friendship and kindness, two girls, Salma and Lily, take us through the process of accepting one another for whom they are.

The main setting for the story *The Sandwich Swap* takes place in the room at school we all remember; a place where friends were made, stories were told and secrets were shared – the cafeteria. Putting ourselves in the places of the main characters, we were quickly brought back in time to those noisy days, sitting on plastic stools among a variety of sights and smells.

Looking back, we all reflected on our favorite brown paper bag lunches that we took to school every day. The most popular sandwiches among members of our group were by far those of peanut butter and jelly as well as bologna with cheese. Oh, the cheese; it was always melted into the mustard or mayonnaise by the time it came time for lunch, but we ate it anyway. After all, what were our options?

The sandwiches that we found most amusing were Gina's bread with butter and Debby's anything sandwich, as long as it was made with round bread.

One of our members is a retired teacher who recalls using books such as *The Sandwich Swap* to teach character traits by embedding examples of positive qualities and behaviors into the curriculum. It is one of many books that can help students grow into trustworthy and responsible people.

We all agreed that as a highly educated society, we want our children to learn everything they can, and not just the "3 R's" of long ago. Reading, writing and 'rithmetic are not enough to prepare our children to be contributing members of society and of the world. Tolerance, acceptance and diversity are important additions to our children's education and the lessons from *The Sandwich Shop* by Her Royal Majesty Queen Rania are ones we hope all schools and families across our country are teaching with great emphasis. In this tale of two friends from different backgrounds, we see that if we take the time to listen and open our hearts and minds to others, we can create a world that is open to an unlimited amount of possibilities.

In addition to *The Sandwich Swap*, there are two other books that we would recommend. Their themes and positive main characters do much to help children see how they can not only improve their schools and communities, but the world.

For the younger crowd, those attending elementary school, we believe an important read would be *The Sneetches* by Dr. Seuss. Behind the wonderful words and rhythmic prose, children can learn about diversity and differences and how to become ambassadors of kindness and respect. (We know many teenagers and adults who love this book as well.)

For teenagers, we would recommend *A Tree Grows in Brooklyn* by Betty Smith. It is the inspiring story of a poor young girl, Mary Frances Nolan, who learns to find pleasure and joy in the smallest of things. Students will follow her through her many struggles and learn how one's inner strength can lead to success.

We found the message from *The Sandwich Swap* to be an important one, so we designed a special day to spend with our children and grandchildren by taking the major point of the story and created our own "teachable moment." Following our reading of the story to them, they ventured into the kitchen where they either created their favorite sandwiches to share with someone else, or tried something that another child had made for them.

To our surprise and delight, our lesson on charity and benevolence grew into something for which we did not prepare, the love of writing. We explained to the children that we wanted to spend the day with them by reading a story aloud. We told them about our club and how we loved to both read and write. Hearing us talk about our club and our new writing project left them wide-eyed and thoughtful. Albert Einstein once said, "Setting an example is not the main means of influencing others, it is the only means." And on this particular day, it was. In the days that followed, two of the grandchildren, Kayla and Jackie, having taken our words to heart, produced beautiful poems.

The OBBC gives *Kayla and Jackie* **5** spoons out of **5**.

From The Whine List:

After drinking a glass of *Pennywise Chardonnay*, someone was heard to have said, "Live the simple life!"

THE MORSEL OF THE STORY

Race Car Poem **by Kayla**
(Kayla enjoys going to the races with her grandparents.)

Zooming, Racing, Speeding by,
The sound heard is a vroooom of the engines cry,
When the flag is glided by and the green light goes,
The fans go wild from head to toes.
The cars make their way around the track,
They might never come back!
When a car crosses the finish line it's a cheer and a trophy close in hand,
The crew and the driver are one lucky band.

God's Greatest Gifts by Jackie

(This was a thank you note written to Nana.)

*God's greatest gifts go too often unseen
But, I have found the gift he made for me.*

*I struggled everyday and things began to get hard.
How could I achieve my goals with such a broken heart?*

*My plan to live out my dream began to diminish.
That was when God stepped in and granted my wish.*

*It wasn't a package or money to spend,
It was you … bringing me in and taking my hand.*

*You began giving me a whole new outlook on life,
Taught me happiness didn't need to be an everyday fight.*

*You walked me down a path I could only dream of
When I began to lose direction you gave me a well needed shove.
Helping me take those steps to get where I was going.
I felt happy again and it was slowly showing.*

*The role you began to play in my life was one I didn't expect.
You gave me a sense of family and a love I couldn't reject.*

*You weren't going to let me quit when the going got tough,
And for this Nana, I could never thank you enough.*

*Whatever my future holds and no matter what I come to do
I will always remember I am where I am because of you.*

*I have been given an opportunity that I almost missed.
Therefore I'm one of those people who have been truly blessed.*

THE MORSEL OF THE STORY

Wanting to put what they learned from **The Sandwich Swap** *into action, the kids created sandwiches they hoped everyone would like.*

After lunch, the children enjoyed crafting.

Tea anyone?

PINKIES UP, PLEASE!

Wanting to read and discuss a "classic," we certainly had a long list from which to choose. We decided on *Emma*, a brilliant comic literary work by Jane Austen. We were drawn to this classic because it seemed very much like a 21st century television reality show, as it dealt with Emma Woodhouse's day-to-day existence at parties, picnics and teas. *Emma* contains all of the elements that people like to see in these "real-life" three act stories of conflict and resolution; being first introduced to a problem in Act I, seeing the problem worsen in Act II, with a "big twist" resolution occurring in Act III.

The dominant theme of *Emma* is marriage, and all of the major activities of the novel revolve around marriage and matchmaking. In "Act I," Emma believes that she has found her purpose in life as a matchmaker. Following the success she had by finding the perfect match for her former governess, she believes that she can make a match between anyone. But in "Act II," the good intentioned Emma finds she is really not good at matchmaking at all. Her only real success is wrongly meddling in other people's affairs. Finally in "Act III," Emma stops spending time on worrying about the feelings and relationships of others, and concentrates on herself. Only in the end she is able to find her own true love with a man she felt was promised to another. "It darted through her mind with the speed of an arrow that Mr. Knightly must marry no one but herself."

In her effort to create romance among the people in her life, Emma fashioned a number of parties which became significant events of not only the social interactions of the period, but to a great extent, contributed to the theme of this tale.

These English parties seemed so festive and beautifully formal that they presented for us something we wanted to try to emulate. So in the spirit of nineteenth century England, we broke from our traditional meeting place, (one of the club member's living rooms), and held a harvest tea party.

Menu

Sandwiches and Savories

Cucumber Sandwiches w/ Mint Butter

Walnut Tea Sandwiches

Carrot Raisin Tea Sandwiches

Petticoat Chicken Cups

Austen-tatious Oysters

Breads w/Clotted Cream & Lemon Curd

Fruits

Strawberries and Balsamic Vinegar

Keepsake Apple Dip

Sweets

Melt in Your Mouth Scones

Tropical Cherry Sweet Cakes

Sacred Triple Chocolate Brownies

CUCUMBER SANDWICHES WITH MINT BUTTER

¼ cup butter, softened

2 Tbs. fresh mint leaves, chopped

8 very thin slices white bread, crusts removed

½ large English cucumber, peeled and thinly sliced

In a small bowl, combine butter and mint. Spread the mint butter on the bread slices. Lay cucumber on four of the slices and top with remaining bread to make four sandwiches. Cut in half diagonally and then in half again.

WALNUT TEA SANDWICHES

1½ (8oz.) pkgs. cream cheese, softened

½ cup ground walnuts

2 Tbs. finely-minced fresh parsley

1 Tbs. finely-minced green bell pepper

1 Tbs. finely-minced onion

1 tsp. freshly squeezed lemon juice

¼ tsp. nutmeg

salt and pepper to taste

24 slices white bread or tea sandwich bread

½ cup unsalted butter, softened

In a large bowl, combine cream cheese, walnuts, parsley and bell pepper. Add onion, lemon juice, nutmeg, salt and pepper. Stir until well blended. Spread one side of piece of bread lightly with butter. Top buttered side of 12 slices of bread with some of the cream cheese mixture and top with remaining bread slices, buttered side down. Carefully cut crusts off from each sandwich. Cut the sandwiches in half diagonally and then cut in half again. If desired, decorative shapes can be made with cookie cutters.

CARROT RAISIN TEA SANDWICHES

1 cup grated carrots

8 oz.(½ can) prepared cream cheese frosting

8 oz. cream cheese, softened

¼ cup finely chopped walnuts or pecans

4 slices cinnamon raisin bread

In a medium bowl, combine carrots, frosting, cream cheese and chopped nuts. Spread one side of two slices of bread with carrot frosting mixture (about ¼ - inch thick). Top with the remaining slices. Carefully cut off crusts from each sandwich. Cut the sandwiches in half diagonally and then cut in half again. If desired, decorative shapes can be made with cookie cutters.

PETTICOAT CHICKEN CUPS

½ cup chicken (white and dark), minced
¼ cup + 1 Tbs. sesame oil
1 celery stick - julienne strips
1 large carrot - julienne strips
small head Boston or lettuce of choice
radicchio lettuce – small amount
10 - 12 cherry tomatoes (quartered)

2 scallions (green onion) - chopped
3 pkgs. Ramen noodles (chicken flavored)
fresh parsley to taste – minced
fresh grated parmesan cheese for garnish
1 - 2 Tbs. Tamari sauce
salt and pepper

Break up noodles into pieces. Boil noodles until done – do not overcook. Cool and mix well with sesame oil enough so noodles are coated and not sticking together. Cool to room temperature. Marinate chicken with Tamari sauce, salt and pepper for 1 hour. Grill chicken until done, approximately 5 minutes on each side. Set aside to cool. Slice carrots, celery and green onion into julienne strips. Cut cherry tomatoes in quarters. Mix noodles and veggies and add 2 envelopes of dry chicken flavoring (included with the Ramen noodles) with ¼ cup of sesame oil. Grind chicken to a minced consistency. Fill each muffin cup with 1 leaf of each type of lettuce then add noodle mixture and place chicken on top. Garnish with cherry tomato and sprinkle parmesan cheese on top. Serve at room temperature.

AUSTEN-TATIOUS OYSTERS

1 pt. fresh or frozen oysters, coarsely chopped

2 cups saltine cracker pieces

¼ cup butter, melted

½ tsp. salt, dash of pepper

½ cup milk

Combine oysters with their liquid. Mix cracker pieces with melted butter. Arrange half of mixture in buttered shallow baking dish. Pour oysters in layer. Sprinkle with salt and pepper. Pour milk over all. Bake at 400 degrees for 20 minutes or longer if crispness is desired.

STRAWBERRIES AND BALSAMIC VINEGAR

fresh strawberries
½ cup good quality aged balsamic vinegar
1 cup powdered sugar

Place strawberries, vinegar and powdered sugar in separate bowls. To serve, dip a strawberry into the balsamic vinegar and then into the powdered sugar.

KEEPSAKE APPLE DIP

1 cup brown sugar
½ stick butter
2½ oz. sour cream

2½ oz. cream cheese
(melt in microwave before adding)
1 tsp. vanilla extract
apple slices

Melt brown sugar and butter together in a saucepan over medium heat. Add sour cream, cream cheese and vanilla. Cook all ingredients on stove until it comes to a bubbling boil. Remove from heat, cool and refrigerate about 2 hours before serving. Serve with a variety of sliced apples.

Pinkies Up, Please!

The Queen and her Lady in waiting.

Planning for our harvest garden tea went beyond preparing the food. This was a very special occasion for us, complete with period costumes and various activities to represent some of the themes of the book.

Like the Regency Period of Jane Austen's era, we learned the importance of tea time in the middle of day. Therefore, we began our afternoon experience with a game involving tea. Upon arriving to Laurie's home, we secretly set out a sample of our favorite tea. By doing so, we created a game to guess which tea belonged to whom. There was a three-way tie among our ladies who successfully made the correct matches. The only way we could think of breaking the tie and declaring a winner was with a game of Old Maid. So by her lack of expertise at this Victorian card game, Deb became the "Old Maid" and was awarded a new teapot.

After crowning our "queen of the teas," we ventured out to the garden for an elegant luncheon. And to work off our calories we engaged in a friendly game of croquette.

The Morsel Of The Story

Pinkies Up, Please!

And lastly, since match-making was the all-encompassing theme of *Emma*, we decided to do a little match-making of our own. We each brought a picture of our "dream date," hidden in a sealed envelope, and placed it in a special basket by the entrance. As we departed from this day's nostalgic event, we picked from the basket the "match" that would accompany us home.

Who's your dream boat?

And lest we forget......After drinking a glass of *La Di Da Sweet Red*, someone was heard singing, "Match-maker, match-maker make me a match."

Pinkies Up, Please!

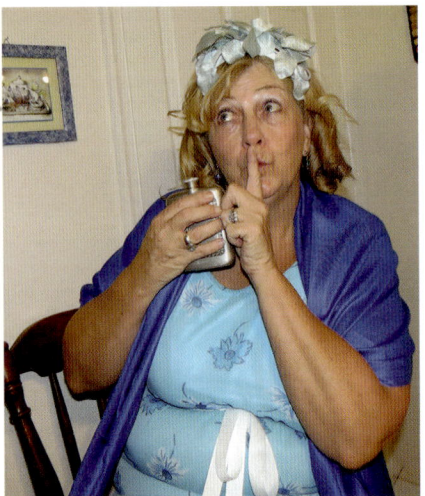

The Morsel Of The Story

154

Pinkies Up, Please!

Not all of the ladies were on their best behavior.

The Morsel of The Story

The Leftovers

Front row left to right – Cheryl Proudfoot, Laurie Cazille and Sue Young

Second row left to right – Gina Hove, Deb Patton, Euna Scott, Kelly Keyes, Donna McElwee and Cheryl Laurento

"The Groceries"

"One Nanny and one old goat!"

"Popcorn Queen"

"Just goes to show ya"

Leftovers

"Secrets are no good."

"Bruce is on the loose. Is it big Bruce, little Bruce or local Bruce?"

"Parsley, Sage, Rosemary and Thyme."

"Knitted Plastic Bags"

"He's alive!"

"Right here. Right now!"

"Sad...beginning middle, end."

"......stays in Vegas."

"Loser..a varsity loser."

"Oldest OBBC Member"

"Youngest OBBC Member"

"Ei8ht!!!!!!!" –

"It tastes like peach pie to me... and the cookies are angry."

"Sparkle Farkle!!"

EDITORS

As the Beatles would say - *"It's been a hard day's night!"*

The Morsel Of The Story

"Some – ting- wong?"

Editors

Celebrating . . . finally we read again!

OBBC Kitchen

Austen-Tatious Oysters 144
Backup Apple Crisp 117
Busy Day Chicken 55
Carrot Raisin Tea Sandwiches 142
Chair Man's Lemon Trifle 91
Christmas Salsa 32
Clued-In Jell-O Salad 56
Collector's Baked Beans 71
Common Dahl Dip 27
Cornfield Chowder 79
Cucumber Sandwiches with Mint Butter 140
Dale's Breakfast Delight 81
Drive Thru Lemon Sponge Pie 116
Edward's "Red Hot Mushroom" Turnovers 8
Elsie's Luncheonette 98
English Toast Casserole 115
First Date 70
Forbidden Dessert 11
Friday Night Special 10
Game Day Veggie Burgers 54
Hero Bacon Quiche 72
Holiday Chicken and Rice 33
Insane Artichoke Dip 124
James' Special Slaw 114
Keepsake Apple Dip 146
King's Roast on Toast 82
"Locks" Cheesy Rounds 17

Mellow Yellow Chicken & Squash	125
Melt in Your Mouth Scones	108
Millie's Molasses Cake	49
Oatmeal Dip and Honeydew Melon	39
PB & G Bar Cookies	41
Pepperoni Potato Casserole	89
Petticoat Chicken Cups	143
Pizza Dip Eclipse	9
Plantation Cornbread and Cheese Casserole	47
Postman's Pasta Bake	73
Quiche La Cle	18
R & C Seafood Chowder	106
Reb's Seafood Pasta	40
Sacred Triple Chocolate Brownies	107
Santa's Jingles	34
Shore Crab Dip	69
Six Pack Punch	80
Smokehouse Casserole	48
Snicker Brownies	57
Stottsville Graveyard Pudding	83
Strawberries and Balsamic Vinegar	145
Tatted-up Coffee	97
Tiramizoe	19
Tropical Cherry Sweet Cakes	28
Tumbon	90
Twisted Pretzel Pineapple Salad	126
Walnut Tea Sandwiches	141

THE END